A CAREFUL DISORDER
Chronicles of Life, Love and Laughter

25th December 1987

For Tisha and Donald —

With the warmest Regards,

Steve

A CAREFUL DISORDER
Chronicles of Life, Love and Laughter

by

Stephen Vicchio

Christian Classics, Inc.
Post Office Box 30
Westminster, Maryland 21157
1987

First Published 1987

© 1987 by Stephen J. Vicchio
ISBN: 0 87061 135 6
Printed in the U.S.A.

To Gwinn Owens,
fine writer, wise editor, gentle friend.

The majority of men are subjective toward themselves and objective toward all others, terribly objective sometimes, but the real task is in fact to be objective toward oneself and subjective toward all others.

Soren Kierkegaard

Table of Contents

A Careful Disorder: xiii
a Kind of Introduction

Childhood

My Father's Hands 3
Losing Things 6
Redemption in School 9
The Liberty 12
Fish Memory 15
The Right Spot 17
The Secret 20
The Pratt Street Boogie 23
    and Other Madness
The Fourth Wise Man 31

Religion

A Conversation on Mount Sinai 34
The Hans Kung Case 38
In Which Creation do 42
    Creationists Believe?
Who Sees Electric Jesus?: 46
    Some Comments on *Joe Egg*
No Word from God on the ERA 49
Embracing the New Lepers 52
The Charles Curran Controversy 57
Faith, Ambiguity, Wonder: 62
    Some Comments on *Agnes of God*
Nobody Left in School 67

Death

The Cold Breath of Dachau 73
Death on the Coffee Table 76
A Sister Died 78
The Frank Coppola Case 81

One Last Mad and Decisive Act 87
Scrooge and Marley: 92
    Partners in Death
Dancing with Death 95
Free at Last 97

Travel

Love, Y.B. 101
Where the Heavens Meet the Sea 104
X,Y,Zed 106
Cairo: Land of *Kismet* 108
Ambience 112
The Pyramids — From a Couch 114
Broken Things 116
Minding My Queues 118
Life and Death in Scotland 120

Science

Theology as Biology 123
The Karen Quinlan Case 128
Mimeograph Mitosis 133
Aerial Criticism 136
Matters of the Heart 138
The Baby Fae Case 142
The Mary Robaczynski Case 146
Psychologist at Work 150
Of Plastic Hearts 153

Academia

Epitaph for a Teacher 159
Terminal Case of Love 162
Camus' Philosophy: VARROOOOM! .. 165
May's End 168

Take a Philosopher to Lunch 170
Grad Speaker Available 173
Scatology and Eschatology 176
Die Fliegen 178
Philosopher's Mall 181

The Bomb

The Dragon and the Turtle 185
No Man will Venture Farther 189
Hiroshima: Nightmare of War 192
    to Nightmare of Peace
The Dancing Class of 199
    Nuclear Initiative
On a Tiny, Fragile Planet 202
Nothing 205
Moral Forgetting 208

Vagrant Thoughts

Gifts of the Fall 213
Annual Lamps 215
Intermolecular Spaces and 218
    Boardwalk Cracks
Observing Aurora 221
Taking Christmas too Seriously 223
Margaret Mead: 226
    Who Fells this Redwood?
Loneliness 229
Caught Underwears 231
Readers of Messages 234
The Self Advertisement Hall of Fame . . 237
Mundane Mysteries 240
At Last, Renewal 244

A Careful Disorder:
a Kind of Introduction

> There are some enterprises in which a
> careful disorderliness is the true method.
> -- Herman Melville
> chapter 82, *Moby Dick*

The writing of introductions is not an easy matter. It is a kind of backwards affair: one spends several months, or perhaps years, putting together a book. After the project is complete, the writing of a suitable introduction looms as a daunting if not impossible task. How does one explain in a few pages what it took hundreds to do? It is important to remember though introductions are read first, as a kind of promissory note, they are inevitably written last, in something akin to the same spirit one examines a bank balance at the end of the month -- the damage has already been done, all that is left is the explaining of it.

What makes the explaining of this book so difficult, so cumbersome and untidy, is that it is a collection of essays, reviews, commentaries, observations and confessions written over the past 15 years. The living of that 15 years has been anything but tidy. Any introduction to the contours of that life, to the gain and loss of love, the struggles and completion of a Ph.D. dissertation, and the ongoing drama of everyday family concerns, would seem facile, even in the most earnest of attempts at telling it. The secrets and hidden meanings of most lives, I should think, are prime candidates for the object of Ludwig Wittgenstein's aphorism: "About that which you cannot speak, you must remain silent." But still, there is a need to say something about this life and the mind that produced these disparate pieces of prose. It may be of some help in understanding the careful disorder that became this book.

These prose writings come out of a consciousness that to me, its owner, seems as protean and everchanging as the billowy clouds that have just become visible outside the stark, metal-frame window of the airport lounge in which I sit attempting to write. I stare at a blank yellow note pad. I wait for a plane to Baltimore. I wait for the words to come -- words that will explain the life, and thus the book. When one writes, sometimes the words come early. They are like a train making an unscheduled stop.

There is a danger no one will be on the platform to meet them. Sometimes they come late. They are discovered after the piece has traveled to the publisher. These words I now use will have to do. They are written with a line from Joubert in mind: "Words are like eyeglasses. They blur everything they do not make more clear."

For the past 15 years, I seem always to have been going somewhere, sometimes as pilot, more often as passenger. These essays are a log of those travels. They stand as a record of where I have taken my belongings, as well as where my mind has wandered.

These prose pieces make whistle stops at many of the most important people and places of the last decade and a half: Jim Jones' Guyana, Karen Quinlan's New Jersey and Qaddafi's Libya. The book makes brief stops at Loren Eiseley's Nebraska, Baby Fae's nursery, and the electric chair in Virginia's Mecklenburg state prison. It visits Barney Clark's plastic heart, Margaret Mead's Samoans and Elisabeth Kubler-Ross' dying patients. As you will see, these and many other sites have been part of the landscapes, both inner and outer, I have traveled in those 15 years.

This book is also about the more distant past. It visits the pyramids of Cheops and Chepren, Captain Cook's Antartica, Borman, Lovell and Anders' trip to the moon, Dickens' London, the death camp at Dachau, and the events of Hiroshima in August of 1945. In many of these pieces I try to make some honest if nevertheless meager observations about important times and places now only the province of a sometimes not so careful memory.

These essays are also an account of many lesser known people and places. In these pages you will find the two craziest people I have known. You will be introduced to street people, parents, siblings, hair weave salesmen, and a group of construction workers musing over the finer points of nothing. You will find underwear thieves, grandparents, students, colleagues and a thoughtful nun from the sixth grade.

More than anything else, you will begin to see, I hope, this book works as a collection of maps. Some are for territories traveled by us all. Though these paths are sometimes well worn, it still may be valuable to see what a fellow traveler has to say about the trip. Other maps are interior, the territory of personal memory. They are no more alike than the contents of any two human minds. This book, if it works, functions as a collection of maps of an individual consciousness, public and private. It is a somewhat incomplete and peripatetic record of what it is like to live and think in the Western hemisphere in the 1970's and 80's.

The collecting of the pieces of this life came about at the suggestion of John McHale, the publisher at Christian Classics. He has given me constant encouragement and support. My gratitude goes to Mary Catherine Sacco who worked very hard in the typing and organizing of the manuscript, to Erika Scheuer for careful copy editing, and to Joyce Seckinger who spent many hours in the typesetting of these words. A special word of thanks must also be extended to my dear friend

Susan Howard who edited and designed the book, to Toni Adashi for alerting me to the existence of the extraordinary woodcuts I have included in this volume, and also to my colleague and friend, Josephine Trueschler, for reminding me about the opening lines of Chapter 84 of Melville's *Moby Dick*.

Finally, I must pay a special debt of gratitude to Gwinn Owens of the *Baltimore Evening Sun*, who in his years as editor of the op-ed page taught me much about how to be a writer some day. It is to him this book is dedicated.

Many of these pieces first appeared in the *Baltimore Sunpapers, The National Catholic Reporter, The City Paper, Commentar, Today* and *Newsday*. I am grateful, particularly to Mike Bowler and Ray Jenkins of the *Evening Sun*, for their permission to reprint them here.

Baltimore, August, 1986   S.J.V.

CHILDHOOD

*Childhood is measured out by sounds
and smells, and sights before the dark of reason grows.*

-- John Betjeman

My *Father's Hands*

I awoke one morning to discover I have my father's hands. I don't know how it happened. I was standing at the mirror and, while sleepily staring through morning shaving cream and bathroom steam, there they were -- my father's hands were shaving my face. I put the razor on the basin and peered incredulously at them. It was undeniable. They were my father's hands.

I recall when I was no more than seven or eight years old. On Saturday mornings my father would take me for visits to his old neighborhood. On the way, we would sit alone, often in silence, and I would secretly stare at his hands. No one had a pair of hands like those. They were large and strong with nails full of the previous day's work. He had a habit of driving with his right hand gripped at the top of the steering wheel, the left arm propped at the open window. The long fragile ash of a neglected Chesterfield regular usually dangled between the index and middle fingers of his left hand. Sometimes I would stare at the precarious ash, wondering when it would make its anonymous descent to the floor below. More often, I would gaze at the mystery embodied in my father's hands.

When I was 13 or so, in the summers, I began to work with my father's roofing company. My father's business had always been a firm whose members could be easily counted on the digits of one of his tar-stained hands. Sometimes I would stop in the middle of working and stare at those hands. They were fast and clever and as strong as a 13-year-old imagination could make them. The palms were full of enormous, bleached-yellow callouses. Those hands never seemed to make a shoddy or wasteful move.

By the age of 18, I had begun to admire those hands from a distance. Perhaps it would be more accurate to say I loathed and feared those hands more than anything else. Early adulthood sometimes has a way of convincing us that parents are creatures from whom we must create distances by manufacturing differences worth harboring.

It was also in those years that I began to realize how much like my father's handshake mine had become. Each was the kind of grip to which Emerson referred when he wrote, "I hate the giving of the hand unless the whole man accompanies it." In my early 20's, we rarely saved that sure grasp for each other.

A few years ago, my father and I traveled together to the funeral of one of his closest friends. The dead man had burned both ends of the candle until all that remained was the frayed wick of a soul incapable of sustaining light. My father and I sat in his car in the cemetery. A gentle drizzle periodically turned the windshield to frosted glass until made clear again by persistent wipers. The process of obscurity and clarity, obscurity and clarity, continued as the line of cars moved slowly in the direction of the grave site.

My father had been greatly shaken by the death. Carl Jung writes in his journal of arriving at a certain age and experiencing a secret shudder at the death of a close friend. He points out that one begins to add and subtract the days turned to years. It is a matter of simple arithmetic most of us avoid until it is undeniably thrust upon us.

While waiting, we sat in our usual silence. Finally, I hesitantly reached over and touched his hand resting on the seat between us. I said something clumsy about loving him and wanting the moment, despite its sadness, to never go away. Across the distance of a generation, he squeezed my hand. I looked down at his fingers which, for the briefest of moments, covered my own. I thought about Albert Camus' observation in *The Fall* that by a certain age we are all responsible for the faces we own. It is just as true of hands.

I now sit at a typewriter and watch as hands move swiftly across lettered keys. My father has never used his hands for this purpose. He has also never taught Plato or Aristotle or the works of Immanuel Kant. My hands no longer have the hard-yellow callouses developed in a distant but well remembered summer sun. And yet, as I stare at the fingers gliding across these lettered keys, I am conscious of those strong hands I admired as a child. My hands are no smaller than those. And clearly, they are no larger.

Baltimore Evening Sun, December, 1985.

*L*osing Things

I cannot remember when I began to lose things. I guess you could say I have lost it. That time and place are locked away somewhere -- perhaps trapped in a musty pullman's trunk full of neurons and synapses. I can recall, however, that a few weeks before my fifth birthday my mother sat me down in the kitchen to tell me I had lost my grandfather. A few days later, we began making weekly trips to the cemetery. Six feet of black earth and a large bronze marker rested on his sleeping chest. At the time, I did not think we had lost him. I was sure I knew precisely where he was. It was a mystery to me why others did not.

In early adulthood I took less frequent trips to my grandfather's grave. I stopped those visits altogether the day I realized I had somehow lost the reason for going. Occasionally, I rediscover it. Sometimes it is found in a box of old photographs kept beneath my mother's bed.

A few years after I lost my grandfather, my mother began sending me to the store for a few things. By then, I had already managed to misplace several parentally signed test papers and pain producing report cards. My mother would carefully pin to the inside of the breast pocket of my Catholic school shirt the money for groceries. I was always dismayed at the disappearance of the $5 bill in the time it took to get from my mother's kitchen to the Penn Fruit a few blocks away. I often stood in the store, a nondescript building which looked more like an airplane hanger than a supermarket, and check and recheck my pockets. Hope mixed with equal parts of fear until the realization came. The money had vanished, but the grocery list, which my mother had securely fastened to the inside of my other shirt pocket was always right where she had placed it. By the time I had reached the third grade, I was no longer astounded by the loss of grandfathers, money securely pinned to the inside of shirt pockets, or anything else for that matter. Quite early in life, I had dimly suspected the awesome transitoriness of people and things.

Since that time, I have managed to lose toys, baseball bats, my mother in various department stores, lacrosse sticks, wallets, library cards, innocence, books, contact lens, car keys, overcoats, virginity, student papers, credit cards, self respect, concert tickets, one sock of many pairs, lecture notes, loved ones, scholarly papers, and dozens of forms from the dean's office.

It has only recently become clear to me, however, that one of the most difficult things about being human is knowing when to stop looking for things. There are those things one clearly will never find, like contact lens and virginity. When you lose them, you only search in a perfunctory way. One becomes resigned in short order to the notion they are lost forever. There are others, like reading glasses and self-respect, for example, which are usually only temporarily misplaced. If one waits long enough, they usually find you. They most often turn up in the most unlikely of places. It is best to forget about these things completely until they make their reappearance.

But there is a third class of lost things: favorite books, certain abilities and virtues, faith, that one continues to search for but with the sobering suspicion they are never to be found. It seems important to search for them anyway.

It is often in these things, or the longing for these things, one can see the delicate balancing of human hope and fear. It is about these things that a final settling of accounts is often deliberately, carefully avoided. There are some things lost that are so important the admitting of their absence constitutes the loss of too vital a part of the self. It is about these things Emily Dickinson speaks when she reminds us:

Hope is a thing with feathers
That perches in the soul,
And sings the tune without the words
And never stops at all.

Unpublished, 1985.

Redemption in School

We are in the midst of national education week and I can count the number of good teachers I have had on one hand. They are a rare breed, perhaps an endangered species. By the end of the first grade I had dimly begun to understand: there was no place for serendipity in American education. Those who looked too hard for it soon became discouraged. By the middle of the second grade I had the entire process figured out: it didn't much matter what you studied, as long as you didn't like it.

Isadora Duncan once wrote,"The goal of the American teacher seems to be to endeavor to reduce the pupil's senses until almost nothing remains." If you grew up in American schools in the 1950's and '60's, as I did, it is hard to find fault with her analysis. The time in my parochial school was measured in terms of cold war atomic bomb practices, which involved "ducking and covering" under our wooden and wrought iron desks, while we waited patiently for annihilation, and trips to the tiny, black-topped parking lot equipped with white circles for dodge ball. In the infinite stretches of time between these events, we learned: the Palmer method, anti-communist civics, and, from a geography teacher, that Istanbul and Constantinople were twin cities like Minneapolis and St. Paul.

My first-through-the-fifth grades were spent mostly in the principal's office or staring at the many profoundly interesting squirrels that always seemed to congregate just at eye level outside my classroom window, for the purpose of performing acrobatic feats as yet unknown, even to the flying Wallendas.

I was too early to be called a "behavioral problem" or "learning disabled." I was just slow enough in speech to be thought of as "dumb." James Harvey Robinson once remarked, "Teaching may hasten learning." But what Mr. Robinson forgot to tell us is that it may also maim it, kill it outright, or sometimes just render it comatose for extended periods of time. By the first day of the sixth grade, I was working on a flat EEG.

But this initial day of grade six changed my entire attitude toward school, and I suppose when I think about it my disposition toward life as well. I might regress a moment and tell you that this particular day in question did not start out quite so auspiciously. I began the morning by lining up for mass with the fifth graders. I had done so poorly the year before, I was convinced the authorities had made some sort of drastic mistake, an accounting error perhaps, obviously related to the little boxes on the back of my report card indicating I had been promoted to grade six.

It was during recess that same day when the strange thing happened. My new teacher, Sister Redemptina, a statuesque and beautiful nun, pointed her finger at me, in a way that only 1950's nuns could, indicating she wished to see me immediately. I felt my heart begin to race as it seemed to slide up into my throat. I had spent a grand total of three hours in the sixth grade, and now they were sending me back -- right in the middle of dodge ball.

"Stephen," she said evenly, "I want to tell you how happy I am to have you in my class." I glanced furtively over my shoulder to discover if the nearly perfect Stephen Brooks -- the only other boy in my class named after the first martyr -- had mysteriously materialized behind me. He had not. She was speaking to me.

The conversation continued, and by the time the bell sounded my head was swimming, but my heart had returned to its rightful place. Sister Redemptina had redeemed my sense of wonder, right in the midst of darting ten-year-olds, skinned knees and so much lack of imagination. We moved back *en masse*, but in line, to our classroom, where I found myself sitting up a little straighter. The squirrels were on recess. They stayed that way.

About six years ago, on a chilly day in May, I sat with several of my friends under a large maple tree on the campus of a large eastern university. The following afternoon, I was to graduate. We were ruminating, the way graduate students often do, about our intellectual influences: Plato, Aristotle, Pascal, Kierkegaard, and a nun in the sixth grade.

A few days later, I returned to my old grade school. Sister Redemptina was gone. Predictably, everything seemed much smaller, with the possible exception of my imagination.

Someone had saved that in the sixth grade.

Henry Adams once wrote: "A teacher affects eternity; he can never tell where his influence stops." I think Henry was right.

Baltimore Evening Sun, November, 1982.

The Liberry

> All that mankind has done, thought, gained or been: it is lying as in magic preservation in the pages of books.
>
> *--Thomas Carlyle*

Liberry. It was not a word I had heard in the first five years of my life. My grandmother was taking me there. For many months before that day, she had patiently, methodically, taught me to read. Every Saturday we would spend the morning making letters which made words which formed paragraphs. It was very difficult work but rewarding, for it all went into the understanding of the books she had brought to my home: the Hardy Boys, *Coral Island,* Jules Verne, and much more. But now we would travel to the liberry, a place, she said, that housed more books than I would ever be able to read.

The building was a nondescript two story brick structure on Loudon Avenue -- a street that dead-ended, appropriately enough, in cemeteries at both ends. My paternal grandfather lies buried in the one to the north. My bookish grandmother's husband, her partner for 30 years, lies interred in the graveyard at the foot of the street. To this day I cannot think of Huxley's *The Devils of Loudon,* a book I first read while stretched out one summer day on the cool of the library's linoleum floor, without thinking of that quirky and homely West Baltimore branch of the Enoch Pratt Library.

I remember being amazed that first day by the number of volumes. Two floors, several rooms a piece, filled with book-lined shelves. But I was even more astounded that day by the mystery of the Dewey-decimal call letters on the spine of each book. My grandmother explained they were a kind of magical system for keeping track of where each volume could be found in the library.

My grandmother was, of course, correct as usual. There is something about books, and the places where those books live, that is akin to alchemy. Libraries have a magical character that allows us to raise our imaginations to the height of what is most noble, honest and felicitous about human beings. Books have the ability, though we the readers may be poor and unknown, to provide us with the companionship of the wisest and most profound thinkers in every age and place. Erasmus, the great 16th century scholar, had a firm understanding of the power of books. While a young monk, he wrote a letter to a friend: "When I get a little money, I buy books. And if any is left over, I buy food and clothing." Charles Lamb, the English essayist and critic, tells the story of a book lover who desired his coffin be made from the strong shelves of his library. My grandmother's devotion to books was no less intense.

I learned much from my grandmother's reverance for books and the buildings in which they are kept. It was as if she did not really believe there are such things as books, only minds alive on the shelves. They lie sleeping until awakened by the touch of a reader. Then, each book speaks in its own recognizable voice. Sometimes those voices traverse great distances in time and place, and yet, if they are good books, the voices are clear and distinct. Although the voices may be as different as Shakespeare and Singer, Melville and Malamud, they are also alike in that they all speak of stories that are truer than if they really happened.

To paraphrase Edward P. Morgan, books and libraries are places where a fragile thought may be examined without breaking it, where an explosive idea can be looked at without it blowing up in one's face. More than anywhere else, they are places where one may find both intellectual provocation and intellectual privacy.

My grandmother, a woman who some would say did very little traveling, understood that people who make use of a good library have lived far more than those who cannot or will not read. It is simply false that we have but one life to live. If we are near a library we may live as many lives, and as many kinds of lives, as we desire.

Some time ago, I returned to the old library on Loudon Avenue. Large pieces of ply wood covered the Georgian windows through which I had gazed as a child, watching the progress of grey, curl-tailed squirrels climbing the oak in front of the red brick building. Now, life was gone from the yard, and the library as well. The books had been moved, the library closed down.

In a real way, that small ghost of a library is like the cemeteries at either end of Loudon Avenue. The voices have been stilled. Life is gone from those places, but not lost. Those of us touched by the dead sleeping in the dust of those grave yards carry them around in our hearts and minds. Their voices can be heard there. Thomas Carlyle once wrote: "Books too are about the human heart and its passage through time." For 30 years now, I have carried those voices with me, and the memory of the building in which they once lived.

Today, Fall, 1986.

Fish Memory

My memory has little talent for taking photographs. It has no knack for storing away experiences -- captured like polaroid snap shots or insects trapped in blown glass -- later to be summoned at will. Instead my remembrances seem more like painted portraits: of a solitary face glimpsed for an instant through the grimy window of a slow moving train; of the bony arthritic fingers of a dying friend; of strangely beautiful landscapes, places of power and forboding, where the earth's first or last inhabitants might be found to dwell.

Sometimes my memory works on these experiences for years, adding and subtracting details, changing tone or perspective, until the completed painting is finally ready to be revealed to my waking consciousness. The unveilings come in many ways. This afternoon I was shown one of those vivid canvases. It appeared while I stood at the seafood counter in Lexington Market. People rushed up and down the narrow concrete aisle next to the small stall. The simple act of holding up a single grey colored fish produced the clearest remembrance of the one tremendous catch I have made in my life.

I was seven years old, away at six weeks of summer camp. The camp was situated by a small clear water lake on the other side of the world from the brick row house I called home during the school year. In school I was slow, ordinary, easy to lose in a class of 50 students. At camp I ran fast, swam well, and hoped the older boys liked me.

That day I had spent the better part of the afternoon standing on the edge of a long wooden pier, borrowed fishing pole in hand, waiting patiently for my first catch. In the early afternoon, the pier had been filled with other campers, mostly older boys, owners of their own tackle boxes. By the late afternoon, only I remained. Patience had turned to skepticism and embarrassment. One was known at camp for the fish one caught.

Finally, long after dinner had closed, and the canteen at the other end of the pier had opened, a small, green-speckled fish struck my line. It strained frantically at its submerged end. My skinny arms and shoulders did the same at the edge of the pier. With some great difficulty, I landed the fish. It flapped about with my borrowed hook buried deep in the side of its mouth. I picked it up by its lifeline. It thrashed back and forth in some strange genetically programmed dance with death until finally it hung motionless, life oozing fast from its blood red gills. It was as if it had come face to face with death and was left exhausted and paralyzed by the enormity of the moment.

The fish hung from my hands, cold, lifeless, still. Its sea-green skin was dappled like that of an overripe watermelon. I examined the fish carefully: the razor sharp tail fins; the aching side holes; the eyes, yellow-blue, the color of cataracts; the bones lined up in the V-shaped pattern of my father's enormous grey overcoat hanging in the crowded living room closet at home.

I admired the eyes, now completely dilated, as if wishing to see as much of the end as they could. I stared for a moment longer at the last victory on that long pier. I would take the fish to the older boys. It would be a late victory, but a victory still.

I stared at the fish for a moment longer until it became a mystery. I hesitated. I could no longer hear the untroubled shouts of the older boys in the canteen. Again I stared into the fish's eyes. Death stared back. I removed the hook from deep in its mouth and returned the fish to that small clear water lake in the middle of Carroll County. The splash was not loud enough for the older boys to hear.

Unpublished, 1972.

The Right Spot

Before it was remodeled there was a corner of the Pennsylvania Railroad station where the faint of heart never sat. The sun never shone in that *cul-de-sac*. It existed in the shadows. Its inhabitants seemed to prefer it that way. This section of the station was not frequented by travelers. It was the province of an assortment of bag ladies, police officers, and a certain segment of Charm City's poor who regularly sought refuge there from the weather, or sometimes just attempted to cling to life for a few days more.

The other morning, while sitting in my office, I watched a bewildered fly, numb and forgetful, attempt to gain freedom from a philosopher's study. The hum of summer was at its muted end. The fly had succumbed to six months of gravitational pull. The prospects for its survival were quite slim, and it seemed to realize that my office was not the proper place for a self-respecting fly to do its dying. It lethargically buzzed to and fro for a while until it mustered enough energy to hurl itself several times against the cleanest of my window panes. A few moments later, the fly was dead. It was as if in the middle of its dying it remembered where it was supposed to be.

In the pre-renovated train station, tubercular looking old-men-before-their-time would cling to their seats, like veterans of the first pew of church, they saw something immensely symbolic about those wooden benches they could not easily give up. Now and then these men with ashen faces would sleep, their scarred, grey heads bobbing fitfully, until from exhaustion or drink, they rested painfully on the backs of their wooden spaces.

Once in a while, one of the stubble-faced sleepers would not awaken. Like the solitary fly, there was a desire to die with one's own. Insect and human held on as long as they could. Sometimes they were lucky enough to find the right spot.

We all search for the right spot. But for many of us that place is too far gone, lost, inaccessible. Indeed, the train station has been renovated. Light now shines on the bare pews. Death and camaraderie have been banished from Amtrak -- sent back out in the street. The police make sure it stays there.

All of us search for the right spot. Until we find it, we are lost. We remain disoriented. We experience something of the terror of that solitary fly, trapped, condemned to die with a philosopher. The fly needed to get back to the right place. It is what sends stray cats home from foreign neighborhoods. It points birds north at the first tentative sign of spring. It forces old men to search for one row house in a neighborhood long since vanished.

Some years ago the old Irvington streetcar barn was torn down. Before then, it housed trolleys -- huge, yellow, loaf-shaped hulks of sleeping steel, lined up in rows like bread on a baker's shelf. On the street they became rolling leviathans, their tops spewing forth sparks of electrical life. But inside the car barn, without their Jonahs, they were dormant, inert, still.

As a small school child, I would twice daily carry my blue duffle bag full of brown paper-covered books and parentally signed test papers past the home of the sleeping street cars. Pigeons also lived there -- above, below and between the trolleys -- off-white iridescent purple scavengers. They were fed by the trolley drivers. The birds would feast on the peanuts dropped by unsteady hands, or perhaps kind hands, that had deposited a penny and turned the small metallic crank on the glass and red metal machine just inside the transit company office.

I remember when they demolished the already dilapidated building. It was razed to make room for a small shopping center. The pigeon's eviction notice doubled as a sign announcing the coming of an A&P and a Read's drugstore on that spot. The birds continued to return to that place for several weeks after the car barn was leveled. Then, all at once, they disappeared. But when construction on the shopping center began, they returned for a short time, perhaps until they realized that the new bustle of activity did not mean the return of their former feasts. All that remained for the birds was a rudimentary memory of their former spot, and that seemed quickly to be lost in the exigencies of instinct.

When I was a still smaller child of about five or so, my mother planted a tiny rose bush in the center of our small back yard. Now, almost 30 years later, it is more like a tree. I remember the day she planted it -- her young thin hands placing dirt around the twig of a bush. As it sent tentacles stretching down into the earth, I began to sprout roots through the floor boards of the house. We grew together, twig and boy, tree and man. When my parents leave that house it will be difficult pulling those roots up, though I have not lived there for many years.

Thomas Wolf suggests that we can't go home again. The truth of that statement may lie in the fact that we never really leave it, though we do provide mental renovations whenever necessary. We carry that spot around with us, a kind of chimera, constructed of a curious mix of wants and memories, both accurate and corrected. John Ruskin once wrote, "The home is the place of places; the shelter not only from all injury, but from all terror, doubt and derision." He is speaking of the spot we carry with us. Perhaps the same one glimpsed in the primitive neurons of a frantic fly, the bewildered flappings of some confused pigeons and the fogged musings of a group of bag ladies and derelicts who no longer die in the train station.

Baltimore Evening Sun, September, 1983.

The Secret

When I was a small child, approaching school age, I began to understand that adults were keeping a special secret.

Sometimes in unguarded moments they seemed at the edge of telling it -- that valuable something -- but then would inexplicably change their minds, withdrawing the offer, acting as if there had been no original intention to reveal the mystery. Between playing stick ball on the Penn Fruit parking lot and building forts in the woods near my house, I spent much of my spare time in those early years wondering what the secret could possibly be.

On the way to work Tuesday, while watching three boys crossing the street in the late summer rain, I remembered about the secret. I have by now, mostly by default, joined the ranks of solemn adulthood. What that means in autobiographical terms is that I tend to supply my past with too many athletic victories or comfort myself by clinging to childhood pains, both real and imagined. What it means more practically is that I have become a possessor of the secret.

The first two of the three boys I encountered that morning gave me no cause to think about the secret. They were both about 12 years old and wore the look and clothing of the gangly men/children most American boys that age have become. It was clear by the way they walked and talked this pair was precariously close to learning the secret.

But it was the third boy who reminded me of that one mystery all adults harbor in their souls. He was a child of about six. Baby fat and school yard muscle were just beginning a competition for the determination of the character of his small frame. As he lagged behind the other two, he came close enough to my car so that I could see his stubby fingers wrapped around a "Masters of the Universe" lunch box. The other hand was entwined in the cords of a starched blue duffle bag that was slung over his right shoulder.

In the few minutes I observed him, the boy managed to shift his belongings several times from side to side. He also stopped to tie his shoes, vainly attempted to reconfine his shirttails, which peeked out from under his short yellow raincoat, and yelled to one of the two older boys that if the latter didn't wait up, the little brother was going "to tell."

Big brother and companion continued on ahead. Then the smaller boy defiantly dropped his belongings and yanked off a blue clip-on Windsor-knotted tie. He stared at the tie and then at the brother who by now was way ahead of him.

It was at this point I cleared my throat and rolled down the window. The secret sat dangerously perched on the tip of my tongue, but I hesitated a moment and then swallowed the mystery. The little boy, who had paused for a few seconds to examine me, picked up his tie and the rest of his belongings and meandered across the street with all the *panache* usually reserved for first graders and sometimes the deeply intoxicated.

The secret, of course, is rather disappointing once you know it. It consists of little more than the realization that the job of adults is to get children to learn that at some point in their lives they will be required to do a great number of disagreeable things they really do not want to do. Adults work hard at their job by getting children to do as many unpleasant things as early as possible. Their parents did it to them, and now as adults, like some strange but unyielding manifestation of original sin, they must pass this on to the next generation.

I began to think of all the disagreeable things I do in a given day. This is a pretty sobering thought. I decided I am sorry I know the secret. That's why I didn't tell the boy when I had the chance. But I continued to think about the secret on my way to school. By the time I got to my office I had concluded that most adults really believe that learning to do one unpleasant thing guarantees one's readiness to do a whole host of other unpleasant things. But I think this is untrue. The art of doing unpleasant things, at least for those without the secret, must be learned fresh every time.

Baltimore Evening Sun, September, 1984.

The Pratt Street Boogie and Other Madness

This is about Esther and Straty. She is alive, at least in a manner of speaking. He died a few summers ago. As far as I know, they never met, though they did share something important in common -- they both were hopelessly crazy. I need not launch into a dissertation on the meaning of the word "crazy," or its relatives "mad", "insane", etc. I am not trained for that task, nor do I have any desire to pursue it. It suffices to say both these people, in very different ways, saw the world through what most of the rest of us would call distorted lenses.

I first met Straty in front of the Irvington movie theater, a nondescript building that now houses a faded stucco and wood, store front pentecostal church. I had not yet reached my fifth birthday. My mother was taking me to the barbershop. In the early 1950's, it was the fashion among mothers and barbers to make the head of any five year old boy resemble, as closely as possible, an imperfectly formed cue ball. Eventually, with considerable time but no real effort on the part of the boy, the head would grow to look like an irregularly shaped tennis ball, complete with 1/8 inch of covering fuzz. Whenever my hair was apprehended over the critical limit, an alarm went off in my mother's head, and it was back to Harry's barbershop, a few dinghy store fronts away from the movie theater.

Upon our first encounter of Straty -- I sensed it was my mother's initial meeting as well -- I held tightly to her strong and slender fingers as we walked briskly, our eyes fixed on the melting tar oozing from the cracks in the sidewalk, past this large and very strange balding man. He wore an immense overcoat, even at the height of summer. Large quantities of coarse, bristly black and grey hairs, like strange miniature porcupines, protruded from the vestibule of each ear.

With the aid of a strategically placed piece of wax paper, he managed to fashion a comb into a kind of poor man's harmonica.

His large full lips hummed into the papered comb, producing a limited number of notes. The selection he had chosen for us that morning, I would learn in repeat but not always command performances over the next three decades, was "The Pratt Street Boogie." It was played, I believe, in the key of C, though it is difficult to discern pitch on a wax-paper comb. The lyrics of this tune consisted primarily in a repetition of the line, "I got the Pratt Street Boogie." It was periodically interrupted with a "yeah baby" or two to counteract the obvious tendency toward monotony. These lyrics were delivered in a voice that somehow managed to marry the tone of Fats Domino to the enunciation of Bela Lugosi.

My mother was suitably frightened. I was terrified and strangely impressed. My reaction was something akin to what small children in primitive societies must feel upon their first glimpse of the witch doctor.

As I grew older, I learned Straty was what is referred to in many communities and small towns all over America as the village idiot. He seemed always possessed of an extraordinarily good cheer. (I would learn later, of course, this is one of the sure signs of a certain kind of madness.) This playful, child-like, just short of mischievous nature, combined with an always harmless and vaguely attractive pitch of genuine irrationality, made him a man difficult to ignore.

If it could be said that Straty ever worked, it was at making the lives miserable of those who were employed at the Irvington Rexall Pharmacy. His primary target was an officious and often disagreeable woman who occupied the rung just below that of the druggist in the Irvington Rexall Pharmacy's rather truncated corporate ladder. In her job description was outlined the task of making certain no crazy people bothered the paying customers. Straty made sure she had ample opportunity to exercise her duty. Their relationship was a perfect substantiation of what economists call supply and demand: Straty would supply a major disturbance in the drug store, the woman would demand he leave immediately. That drama repeated itself with all the regularity of the number eight streetcar that stopped just a few paces away.

After high school, I spent the next several years moving in and out of my parents' home. With the movement to and from college, graduate school, and various teaching positions, I made sporadic visits to the neighborhood. In those years it changed dramatically: penny candy stores gave way to pizza places and sub shops, complete with the everpresent odor of fried onions; the number eight streetcar, with electrical life coursing from the lines overhead, was replaced by a habitually late number eight bus; the shoes of born again Christians now stuck to the gum riddled floor of what was once the Irvington theater. But through all these changes Straty remained the one screw-loose but fixed point.

A few summers ago, Straty abruptly disappeared. The usual rumors began. One Saturday afternoon, after looking through the sports pages, I flipped through the obituaries, the only section of the Saturday paper that is ever full size. It was amidst those names lined up in orderly rows, like miniature grave markers, I found the bald madman with the wax paper comb.

He was laid out in the funeral home on Frederick Avenue. Except for a few family members, the room was empty. Everything about the place looked dead, but most of all Straty. His eyes were closed. I had never seen them that way. It was difficult to imagine Straty needing sleep. He was wearing a neck tie. The badly constructed Windsor knot hung around his neck with all the incongruity of high-heeled shoes on a high wire artist. The tie was an unsuccessful attempt at bringing order to an embodied chaos with a wax paper comb. By then, the spirit of that madman had vacated the premises. The hair in Straty's ears was gone. Trimmed. The porcupines had apparently given up their wild habitat in favor of a less domesticated place.

The story of Esther, and her particular brand of madness, is a far different tale. It began to unravel, as she did, about 15 years ago. Before then, she had managed to raise one child to adulthood and to work a good job. She departed each morning from her comfortably furnished row house in west Baltimore and was met by a waiting taxi that drove her to bookkeeping chores in the business section of the city.

In the evening, this neat and attractive professional woman of about 45 would return by cab to the neighborhood, where she was respected for her quiet habits and fine taste in furniture. On the weekends, Esther went out with friends who called on her in Cadillacs and Lincolns. She was always home by a reasonable hour.

But gradually, over the course of several years, Esther began to change. She did not snap. It is no clearer at what point Esther went crazy than when King Lear did. It did not happen all at once. Her illness was more akin to walking down a dark road in a strange land and being too frightened or too proud to ask for directions. In a few years, she would be hopelessly lost.

It began with the burning of a bare light in the living room. It was switched on at dusk and shown brightly throughout the dark hours until made meager by the rising yellow ball that came through her living room window.

Later, Esther traded her purse and attache case for a pair of Holschild Kohn shopping bags. Eventually, she began sitting up all night. The neighbors began to hear a banging sound, like the hanging of pictures, until the early hours of the morning. After a few years, Esther lost her job.

Soon after that, she began breaking up her fine furniture into small pieces. She also methodically placed large sheets of clear, heavy plastic across the stairwells leading to the basement and upstairs. During the day, Esther mostly slept or wrote religious messages, addressed to family members and her former friends, all over her immaculately clean living room walls. The banging sound continued. She had driven 300 four inch nails through much of the floor space of what used to be the dining and living rooms.

In the evenings, Esther illuminated with bare light bulbs the three rooms on the first floor. The rest of the house had been closed off. If THEY were going to get her, she would see them coming. Occasionally, she would howl at a bewildered teenager returning home in those hours when the streets of the city are the province of ragged urban nomads and refugees from last call. When Esther wailed, it was an eerie sound, as if more than one tortured person were screaming from the same pair of aching lungs.

As time went on, Esther disappeared within the first floor of that tiny house for days at a time. The front door had been deadbolted shut. The back door was reinforced with thick sheets of plywood. THEY turned off her water. THEY disconnected the phone. It was about this time, as best we can judge, she decided THEY planned to kill her. She vowed to never leave the house again. If THEY were to kill her, it would be in her own house.

For the next several years, she practiced all the cunning her now 90 pound body could muster. She enlisted the help of two trusted neighborhood children. In the dead of night, she lowered a small plastic bucket on the end of a frayed yellow life-line.

The pail contained money with which the children purchased bread, milk, twinkies, and disposable diapers.

One afternoon, Esther became violently ill. When THEY finally broke in a few days later, THEY found her huddled in a terrified ball in the dark far corner of the only inhabitable room. She was in the throes of a severe ashmatic attack made more complex by malnutrition.

Esther was taken to the emergency room of a local hospital and eventually to a facility for the insane. She carried her shopping bags along. In the mental hospital, she spent her time winding a 500 foot ball of chord around the handles of the two bags. The bags were kept under her bed. The other end of the chord was attached to the bony index finger of her right hand.

During her hospitalization, they fixed Esther's house: walls were painted, nails removed, plywood and plastic was carted away in large yellow trucks. The demons were exorcized.

When the taxi dropped her off at her refurbished home, Esther wore a yellow, polyester suit, with matching handbag. In her other hand could be found the shopping bags, though the string had disappeared.

It was not long, however, before she began to wander aimlessly down that old road. She did not recognize any of the land marks, but she had been through this night journey before. Before long, she covered the stairwells. The howling returned. And the banging. And the bare light bulb. And the thought that at any moment, THEY would break in and kill her.

Esther remains that way today.

Straty and Esther remind us that insanity comes in many

kinds. Some crazy people, like the bald man with the wax paper comb, seem to embrace life so fully and unabashedly that they are essentially undomesticable. Their lives are so full of energy and possibility that single bodies cannot always contain them. The life of Straty was so unfettered, it constantly spilled over into the lives of passers-by. Often, they were not so happy about it.

In centuries past, it might have been said of him that Straty suffered from a divine madness -- a kind of intoxication only to be associated with holy origins. Today, he is explained in less flattering terms, making sure we have made a fine distinction between "idiotic" and "imbecile". But no term, whether pejorative or not, begins to capture the unearthly magic that man generated with nothing more than a pocket comb, a discarded piece of wax paper, and a bit of time on his hands.

If Straty was in some way blessed, Esther may well be cursed -- a curse that also seems to transcend the available explanations of it. Kurt Vonnegut's Dwayne Hoover describe his madness as "bad chemicals in my head." Modern psychiatry attempts to do much the same for Esther, but that explanation somehow seems as narrow as the life it attempts to make comprehensible. Straty's life was so large, it constantly bumped into everyone else's. Esther's become so small its aperture was not wide enough to allow anyone else in.

What we are left with is the rumors about Esther -- not the ghost of a woman who haunts that little brick house, not the frightened, pathetic madwoman who tosses her excrement out the window at night so THEY cannot examine it. The rumors are about the other Esther. They are about the woman who was picked up every morning by a waiting tax, the woman who had three daily newspapers delivered to her door.

Stories are now constructed about Esther in an attempt to discern some order, some teleology that will make sense of the chaos and the pain. When those stories are whispered by the neighbors, they never possess a ring of truth. They say she was brilliant, so brilliant she went crazy. They say she was artistic, and romantic, and unhappy, and much too sensitive for her own good. And this is supposed to bring understanding where there is only madness.

It does not.

Unpublished, 1981.

The Fourth Wise Man

The other afternoon I had occasion to walk through the hall of a small private grammar school. The floors had the shine and smell only small grade schools seem to have. There is something warm but vaguely medicinal about them. White porcelain water fountains cling to the wall just a few feet above the floor. The whole experience gives one the impression of Gulliver happening upon a Lilliputian elementary school in session. The deserted hall gives cause to wonder whether the little people are hard at work or just hiding from the giant.

On the bulletin board was an announcement of the Christmas play to be held in a few days. Memory is a strange depository of sights and smells and sounds. It all gets stored away somewhere. Some of it gets rummaged through and brought back to life. Often it is the seemingly inconsequential that acts as memory's medium.

While standing at the bulletin board I began to recall my first experience in the theatre. It was the Christmas play at St. Joseph's Monastery School, some time in late December, 1956. In those days all Christmas plays were about the birth of the "baby Jesus;" there was apparently something important about the fact He was born a baby like the rest of us.

Boys in my first grade class came in two basic kinds: the tall and the short. They could be further subdivided into the tall smart, the short smart, the tall slow and the short slow. The male hierachy, in the minds of both nuns and children, roughly corresponded to the way they are listed here. I, unfortunately, was a member of the latter group.

This fact had certain repercussions. One of the most important of those was that there were but a finite number of speaking parts in the Christmas play: The tall smart boys became Joseph and the three wise men, who were generally characterized by a profound muteness coupled with a practiced look of reverence; The tall and dumb lads played the roles of shepherds; The very smallest, smartest male, by process of elimination, became the baby Jesus, though this was not, in the strictest sense, a speaking part; This left the parts of various barn yard animals to be played by the short and slow.

In the weeks of rehearsal, I remember appearing for wise men practice. The music sister would quickly count the wise men present, clearly see I was a head shorter than the legitimate kings from the east, and send me back to the collection of small dim-witted boys across the hall learning to moo.

The day of dress rehearsal I was still under the impression the nun in charge of casting had made a profound error in judgment. I was convinced I was the stuff of which wise men are made. By then, I had also grown fond of the idea of presenting the baby Jesus with the "circumstance" that went along with the "gold" and "mud" the other kings carried.

With this in mind, in the midst of dress rehearsal I reared up on my short, bovine hind legs and carried an empty Ru-dots bakery box to the creche, where a surprised baby Jesus seemed awe-struck by the experience. A profound sense of miracle at once pervaded that empty, holly-scented auditorium. It was not just that God became man that Christmas; it was also that cow became King.

Baltimore Evening Sun, December, 1986.

RELIGION

To believe means to recognize that we must wait until the veil shall be removed. Unbelief prematurely unveils itself.

🍎 *-- Eugen Rosenstock-Huessy*

A Conversation on Mount Sinai

The place: Mount Sinai.
The time: late April, 1986.

Moses, looking somewhat younger than his 3,236 years, reaches the summit. He is breathing rather heavily but carries a look of determination on his bearded face. In his hands can be seen two ancient stone tablets. To stage right there is a small sign on which is printed in large block letters: WELCOME TO MT. SINAI/elevation 2,644 meters. On stage left rests a large Coca-Cola machine. Printed on the side of the machine, in bold red and white, is the message: "It's the Real Thing."

Moses: *Elohim...? El Shaddai...? Lord...? Ah...(tentatively) Yahweh?*

God: *(mildly perturbed) I told you not to call me that.*

Moses: *Sorry...sorry. It's just that I'm so upset and confused. I don't know what I'm doing.*

God: *(in a much more pastoral voice) Well, what seems to be the problem, Mo? You know you've always been able to talk to me.*

Moses: *(tentatively) It's about these tablets you gave me.*

God: *You didn't break them again, did you?*

Moses: *No, no, nothing like that. We're going to need some revisions on the original copy.*

God: *Revisions? What on earth are you talking about?*

Moses: *(pointing emphatically to the tablets) Particularly this number six, "Thou shalt not kill."*

God: *That seems pretty clear to me.*

Moses: *Maybe so, but it's causing an awfully big confusion down here. Some feel it applies to separate sperm and ova, others after the two have been united. Still others reserve it for 20-week* old embryos and up. And some think it applies only from the moment of birth.

God: *Holy cow! (He seems a little embarrassed by this remark.) Ah...I mean this is really a mess. This is not at all what I had in mind.*

Moses: *(sheepishly) Well, that's not all. We also have the problem of poison gas.*

God: *Poison what?*

Moses: *Poison gas. The Geneva Convention states that poison gas is one of the most heinous crimes that can be perpetrated upon human life.*

God: *I'll go along with that...so why do people down there bother to manufacture the stuff?*

Moses: *They make it so it can be used in state-operated gas chambers, because it's the most humane way to kill people.*

God: *But if it's the most heinous crime?...This is all too confusing.*

Moses: *But the real reason I've come today is because of the problem of self-defense.*

God: *The problem of what?*

Moses: *You know, self-defense. The problem is that we just can't figure out what it is anymore. Some think it involves using plastic explosives to blow up people dancing in a discotheque.*

God: *Why is that self-defense?*

Moses: *Because the people who did the bombing were protecting themselves from the thoughts the people who were dancing were thinking.*

God: *But what kind of thoughts could they be thinking in a disco?*

Moses: *Other people think self-defense amounts to retaliating by sending jet fighters thousands of miles to drop bombs on the bad people who were responsible for blowing up the good people in the discotheque.*

God: *But why is that self-defense?*

Moses: *I'm not sure. I thought maybe you would know.*

God: *Did any good people get hurt when the good people sent planes to blow up the bad people who blew up the good people in the discotheque?*

Moses: *Yes, that's part of what we call the "problem of noncombatants."*

God: *Well, what did the good people say when they blew up some good people along with the bad people who blew up the good people who were dancing in the discotheque thinking bad thoughts about the bad people?*

Moses: *They said it was unfortunate."*

God: *Unfortunate?...Yes, yes, unfortunate. This is not at all what I had in mind. We must do something about all this immediately.*

Moses: *Yes, I absolutely agree. In fact, I've been working on a rough draft here of an effective compromise that I think may go a long way in alleviating some of these problems. (He produces a roll of toilet paper from beneath his robe. As he unwinds the paper, he begins to read:)*

"Thou shalt not kill any human entity between the ages of minus four months and 18 years, at a distance of less than 500 yards, except in the case of self-defense, or in those instances when good people blow up bad people who have blown up good people who were thinking bad thoughts about bad people, or in those situations as outlined by the Geneva Convention, see paragraph one, section b, which states 'in the case of those noncombatants living in or near a military installation...'"

God: *Wait...wait... There's just one problem. How are you going to fit all those revisions on one of the stone tablets I gave you?*

Moses: *Microchips.*

God: *This really is not what I had in mind.*

🍒 *Baltimore Evening Sun,* April, 1986.

Note: This piece was written a week after U.S. fighter planes bombed Libya in retaliation for what the American authorities believed was Muammar el-Qaddafi's involvement in the terrorist bombing of a night club in West Germany. Several U.S. servicemen were killed in the German explosion.

The Hans Kung Case

On February 15, 1975, after an inquiry lasting more than six years, the Vatican's Congregation for the Doctrine of Faith declared that certain of the Rev. Hans Kung's theological opinions are contrary to Catholic doctrine. It called on Father Kung, a member of the Catholic theological faculty at the University of Tuebingen, West Germany, to stop propagating these unorthodox views.

The ideas that seemed to bother the CDF the most were Father Kung's position against the infallibility of the Pope, the magisterium's unique role in interpreting matters of faith and the conditions for the valid celebration of the Eucharist.

It is quite odd that it took the Congregation six years to decide that Father Kung's views were incompatible with the official position of the Church. A casual reading of the documents of Vatican II could easily have exposed the essential differences between the two in a matter of hours. Perhaps the length of time is more a testament to the politics of the modern Church than the theological complexities involved.

By waiting several years, the CDF gave the impression of making a studied and deliberate analysis of Father Kung's beliefs. Its real purposes, however, may have been to wait, hoping that Father Kung would "harmonize his opinions with the doctrine of the magisterium."

In the years following this first censure, Father Kung seems to have done little to "harmonize" his opinions with those of the Church. On December 18, 1979, the CDF released a second proclamation stating that "Father Kung had departed from the integral truth of the Catholic faith and therefore could no longer be considered a Catholic theologian or function as such in a teaching role." The declaration went on to cite additional points on which Father Kung's position differed from that of the Vatican. Principal among these were the immaculate conception of Mary, the resurrection of Jesus and the consubstantiation of Jesus with the Father.

Several incidents have occurred in the past five years that have prompted the second declaration. *On Being a Christian,* Father Kung's controversial book in systematic theology, may have been an important element. Two more recent writings, however, *The Church, Remaining in the Truth?* and his introduction to August Hasler's *How the Pope Became Infallible,* both published in 1979, were perhaps the deciding factors. Mr. Hasler's book is a devastating attack on Pope Pius IX, the 19th century originator of many of the doctrines Father Kung is against. Mr. Hasler argues, rather convincingly, that Pope Pius was mentally unbalanced and thus reeled off a series of dubious visions to support his own convictions.

In 1854, Pope Pius established the immaculate conception of Mary as a dogma of the Church. The result was that all Catholics were required to believe that Mary was conceived without original sin. Ten years later, Pope Pius issued his *Syllabus of Errors,* a tract in which he condemns socialism, communism, rationalism, naturalism, the separation of church and state, and freedom of the press. "The Roman pontiff," he said at the time, "cannot and should not be reconciled and come to terms with progress, liberalism and modern civilization."

In 1870, the same pope issued a declaration proclaiming the infallibility of the papacy. This doctrine elevates the pope to the supreme height in questions of faith and morals. It is curious how little discussion is heard in the Church today about where these doctrines have come from or about how much influence this one man, Pope Pius IX, has had on the development of modern apologetics.

The difficulties experienced by Father Kung are the latest in a long series of problems encountered by individual theologians. In this century alone, M.J. Lagrange, Teilhard de Chardin, Karl Rahner, John Courtney Murray and Henri de Lubac have all been censured by the Church.

It is important to understand the basis of Father Kung's rejection of certain of the Church's dogma. Father Kung contends that his position is basically a scriptural one. In a press conference after the first proclamation, Father Kung said, "...where the Bible is concerned, the right stands for dogmatized mythology, the left for total demythology. As a 'theologian of the middle,' I stand between the two extremes...I am a conservative in that I hold fast to the historical traditional of the Bible and the Church; I am a radical in that I insist in going to the roots of that tradition."

Raymond Brown, the eminent Catholic biblical scholar, reviewing *On Being a Christian,* remarked, "...Kung's strength is that he develops his theology out of the Bible. The basis of his thoughts about Christ and the church is critical biblical exegesis, and from that optic he evaluates later theology."

This is not to say that Father Brown agrees with all that Father Kung has to say. In the same review, Father Brown says, "I disagree with Kung on many points." But then he goes on to add: "The best thing that could happen for plain decency, for Kung's theological development, for Catholic scholarship, and the love of Christ, would be an announcement by Roman authorities that, while they may think that Kung is wrong and even dangerous, they plan to ignore all his future publications, leaving his errors to be pointed out by competent Catholic theologians."

The CDF's decision has brought a mood of apprehension to Roman universities both here and abroad. The ruling raises a number of questions about how far Catholic theologians will be allowed to go in their academic pursuits. A Dominician monk I spoke with in Venice last month wondered aloud about working in a framework that would be totally unacceptable in any other scholarly field.

A feeling of gloom was particularly acute among younger members at the Jesuit Gregorian University in Rome where the Rev. Jean Gilot, an archconservative, who for years has responded to Father Kung's position with vitriolic diatribes, makes his home.

A few weeks ago, Pope John Paul II visited the Gregorian for supper. Father Gilot was introduced to the smiling pontiff. "I think we've met before," said the pope. Someone else responded loud enough for only a few to hear, "Sure you have; he's your Grand Inquisitor."

Baltimore Sunday Sun, February, 1980.

*I*n Which Creation Do Creationists Believe?

The story of Kelly Seagrave's fight to force the state of California to rewrite its guidelines for teaching the origin of the universe is a strange, confusing and often ironic one. It is strange and confusing for me because I confess to a certain kind of bewilderment at Mr. Seagrave's insistence -- and I happen to teach the Old Testament. Indeed, when I first learned about the new controversy in California about the biblical account of creation I wondered out loud to which of the biblical accounts Mr. Seagraves was referring.

Among biblical scholars over the last century and a half the application of literary critical methods to the study of the Bible has brought attention to a number of anachronisms, repeated narratives called doublets, seeming contradictions, marked changes in literary styles, vocabulary and syntax. All of this has led most reputable biblical scholars to the opinion that the Torah (the first five books of the Old Testament) is a rich, multilayered document with a very long and complex history.

It is common practice among biblical scholars to suggest there are four strata or documents within Genesis through Deuteronomy which can be seen by noting changes in style and vocabulary, as well as subject matter and theological perspective. Foremost among these changes is the alternation of the name Yahweh (a specific proper name for the god of Israel) and Elohim (a more general term meaning "God.")

When the name "Yahweh" is used in Genesis, Moses's father-in-law's name is Reuel, the name for the sacred mountain is Sinai and the natives of Palestine are called Canaanites. When the term "Elohim" is used the father-in-law of Moses is called Jethro, the mountain is Horeb and the inhabitants of Palestine are Amorites.

This point is significant, for in Genesis 1:1 to 2:3 we find a highly structured, repetitious, semipoetic account of the creation of the universe by Elohim. This is followed, however, by Genesis 2:4 to verse 25 where there appears to be another account of creation in which the deity is Yahweh, the order of events is different and the style is much more prosaic.

Chapter one begins with a progression of creation culminating in verse 26 with Elohim making man in his image and likeness on the sixth day. Chapter two continues by suggesting that "in the day Yahweh made the earth and the heavens" (day two in chapter one), He formed man from dust. It is clear that these two points of view are quite different in terms of chronology, not to mention more subtle stylistic and theological disparities.

Failure to see these differences is also a failure to see that the literature grew in the context of the history of the ancient Jews. It is viewed by both Christians and Jews as "inspired" literature, but how the Bible is inspired is subject to a number of interpretations.

The creationists generally hold that every word in the text was dictated by God to people whose only function was to write it down. Others view inspiration as a process in which people encounter God acting in history through their daily living and respond by developing devotional literature that depicts that response. Some say the Old Testament is written by persons inspired in the same way Shakespeare was inspired -- it flows from the wellspring of human genius. For the devout Jew or Christian the last possibility is not enough, but the first alternative may be too much.

Indeed, the failure of creationists to see the differences in the text brings us to one of the stranger elements the trial calls to mind. Although the creationists claim to want to argue the biblical account(s) on scientific grounds, I think their insistence really teaches us more about the psychology of certain forms of religious belief. When one's faith is essentially nonrational no amount of evidence, scientific or otherwise, can shake that perspective. What can readily be seen by those who let the text speak for itself often becomes clouded for people who have invested enormous emotional capital in the text being perfect.

What is perhaps more interesting, however, is how this essentially nonrational view of life seems to have grown in the 1970's. In order to understand this we need only to examine the three greatest box office attractions of the last decade: *The Exorcist, Jaws* and *Star Wars*. All three films tell a recycled version of the 15th century English mystery play where the demonic is always defeated by a young man of faith. The one element added to these modern dramas is a distrust and lack of appreciation for technological answers to our problems.

In *The Exorcist* the young girl is finally saved by the younger priest-psychiatrist when he dives out the window, leaving his psychiatric techniques behind. The salvation scene in *Jaws* occurs when the young police chief does battle with the demonic shark while the oceanographer, the man who knows all about sharks, stays locked in a cage below the surface. Luke Skywalker, of course, saves the day in *Star Wars,* not by using his technologically sophisticated radar, but rather by "following the force." These films may well reflect a broad concern with the social, political and cultural implications of science, and the Seagraves case may be doing this as well.

One of the principal ironies in the trial is that there may be some long-range implications that even Mr. Seagraves had not planned on. Nearly all religious traditions have stories about the age and origin of the universe. More often than not these stories differ quite markedly from each other. For the sectarian Hindu, the universe is vast and filled with innumerable worlds, heavens and hells. There are tremendous cycles of creation and dissolution, each lasting 4,320,000 years. One can almost envision Hindus with *Upanishads* in hand waiting in line together with Hinayana and Mahayana Buddhists, Confucians, Taoists, Zoroastrians and Flat Earth Society members all waiting for their crack at the biology curriculum. But then these ancient texts also have much to say about physics, astronomy, geology and medicine as well.

The final irony in this case involves the realization that the National Science Foundation, the culprit in many of these textbook disputes, began making its big push to update science curricula in the late 1950's, in the shadow of *Sputnik*. Twelve years later Governor Ronald Reagan of California openly encouraged creationists to sue the state to get creationist ideas into biology textbooks. The immediate effect was the rewording of books teaching evolution so that they presented Darwin's theory as no more scientifically verifiable then the creation story.

In 1978, during Jerry Brown's tenure as governor of California, the textbooks were once again rewritten, this time with no mention of the biblical story. It is the new series of texts that Mr. Seagraves, the 37-year-old publisher of religious books, is fighting to change. Presidential candidate Reagan made some cryptic procreationist comments during his campaign, suggesting there are "difficulties with evolutionary theory." Ironically, at the same time he also signalled his intention to renew the arms race, originally started, of course, by the launching of *Sputnik* in 1957.

🌰 *Baltimore Evening Sun,* April, 1980.

*W*ho sees Electric Jesus?: Some comments on Joe Egg

Gottfried Wilhelm Leibniz, the great 18th century German philosopher, thought this was the best of all possible worlds. He was wrong. Given a few moments, we could all envision a better one. Joe Egg could have had a different life. She could have been "the lovely girl running about." She is not. Instead she is spastic, prone to convulsions, confined to a wheel chair, unable to communicate in any meaningful way. Her insensitive physicians inform us "she is a vegetable."

The doctors, of course, are used to this sort of thing. They tell us that this is the way life is. For most of us, this is not enough. We need reasons for what the Vicar calls "acts of God." We need to know why Joe is the way she is. This incessant drive to make sense out of natural calamities serves as one of the major themes in the play. The play is not about Joe Egg's world. It is about a world in which it is possible for Joe Egg to exist. Each of the characters has an answer. Sheila thinks the child is deserved punishment for her premarital promiscuity. Bri believes that God may be "a manic-depressive rugby footballer." Freddie, the uppercrust socialist, strings together a series of platitudes designed to make sense of the couple's situation. His wife Pam deals with Joe by refusing to recognize her existence telling us in the second act, "I can't stand anything N.P.A.: Non-Physically Attractive." Grandmother Grace is sure it was "the genes on the other side of the family." The Vicar tries terribly hard to portray the Church of England as "a far more swinging scene than you may suppose." He offers the suggestion that the Almighty may cause evil in order to stimulate research. Later he falls back, just as pathetically, on some old and worn theological responses: Joe exists due to the "misuse of human freedom" and because "the Devil is busy day and night."

Many of us use these same platitudes. They seem almost to be a necessity since the alternative is too terrifying for most of us. We are harangued face to face by Bri who taunts us for our failure to face the terrifying alternative.

Peter Nichols, the playwright, calls *Joe Egg* a comedy. The play is full of laughter, but of a mysterious kind. In "Lapis Lazuli" Yeats says, "Hamlet and Lear are Gay; Gaiety transfiguring all that dread." Why should people in the midst of overwhelming adversity laugh? Yeats doesn't say the actual moment of tragedy is funny -- it's the moment that follows. This is the comic moment that Bri seizes. He lives through another of Joe's convulsions, observes himself and his situation, and laughs. What Yeats may be telling us is that in that comic moment Hamlet and Lear, and by extension even Bri, are free: free of evil, free of restraint. Laughter provides a momentary detachment. Greek tragedy always involves an ignominious predicament. The tragic error is not sin, not a conscious action on the part of the hero. It is the mistake of being. It is the mistake of realizing that the world is the way it is -- contingent and flawed. Bri's jokes become his last effort at defying despair.

Hidden among "these jokes" is the truth of the couple's marriage. Bri is clever and highly manipulative. We watch him guessing which emotions will appeal to Sheila most and then pretending to experience them. Simultaneously, he refuses to authentically confront his sometimes silly, desperately lonely, always possessive, and occasionally self-pitying mother. For these and other reasons we are tempted to judge this momma's boy a failure. But if Bri's alleged failure is an open one, Sheila's is covert. Though honestly affectionate, loving and womanly, she often cooperates with Bri in his project to remain a child. She also remains indomitable by refusing to face some facts -- among them that it takes love and God to make miracles and she has only love. At the center of this marriage is a child who lies crumpled and moaning yet using up the union's energy diminishing the capacity of love, and punishing her parents constantly with the absurd unreasonableness of her fate.

Early in the play Bri sarcastically asks the speechless, sightless Joe if she's seen the illuminated statue of Jesus set atop the electricity building as a holiday decoration. Obviously, the retarded girl does not see it. Neither do her parents.

🍎 *Commentar,* Fall 1980.

No Word From God on the ERA

We in America are the products of a Western religious heritage that distinguishes politics from religion. Augustine taught us the difference between the city of God and the city of man, and for most Americans this distinction is constantly reiterated by Supreme Court decisions and the Internal Revenue Service.

Early this month, Sonia Johnson, an active lobbyist for the Equal Rights Amendment, was excommunicated from the Mormon Church. Ms. Johnson commented that her church "does not understand that politics has nothing to do with religion." Unfortunately, she is hopelessly naive.

The Mormons, in fact, always have had a keen and pragmatic sense of the connection between politics and religion. Since the mid-19th century beginnings of Mormonism, the one feature that has kept the Church of Jesus Christ of Latter Day Saints an evolving religion is precisely its political adaptability -- always, however, in the context of continuing "divine revelation."

Joseph Smith, the founder of Mormonism, was the first prophet of the latter days (the days of the restoration of God's priesthood on earth) and since his time, each succeeding president of the church has been a prophet -- and the link between "divine truth" and the Mormon community on earth. This notion of continuing "revelation" has enabled Mormonism to legitimize essential ideological change as America's social and political climate has changed.

A case in point are the "revelations" regarding polygamy. The church announced in 1852 that a "revelation" received some years earlier by Joseph Smith made the practice a divinely inspired form of family organization. In 1879, the Supreme Court rendered a verdict against polygamy in the United States. This left the church in an awkward position. Would they continue to practice polygamy?

In 1890, a "divine answer" was given to Brigham Young's successor, Wilford Woodruff. Woodruff issued a "revealed manifesto" condemning polygamy. This new revelation was unanimously sustained by the General Conference in 1890.

Another interesting example of the political uses of "divine revelation" has occurred more recently. Spencer Kimball, the current president of the Mormon Church, announced in June of 1978 that "all worthy male members of the Church may be ordained to the priesthood without regard to race or color." Before Mr. Kimball's "revelation" there had been a prohibition against blacks as priests. *The Book of Abraham,* one of the three scriptures "revealed" to Joseph Smith, said that blacks -- "the descendants of Cain" -- are "cursed as pertaining to the priesthood."

It is clear that Mr. Kimball's "revelation" offered tremendous potential for social and political change within the church. Besides the obvious repercussions it will have for the relations between the Mormons and black Americans, there have also been discussions in the last year about all-black Mormon congregations and stepped-up missionary efforts in Africa.

It is significant that the official church statement charged Ms. Johnson with "spreading false doctrine and working against church leadership." The words "Equal Rights Amendment" were not mentioned at the trial.

The real issue (as seen by the church) may be that during the closed hearing, Ms. Johnson denied the concept of prophetic office. She may feel that any change on Mormon attitudes toward women must come despite what happens in Salt Lake City. Unfortunately, this puts her in the position of not meeting the requirements of Mormon membership.

Ironically, any change in the church's attitude towards females as priests may come precisely through political activity like Ms. Johnson's within the church. Whether or not Ms. Johnson believes that the divine revelation is vouchsafed in Salt Lake City, one thing is certain: The Mormon's don't believe it is vouchsafed to Ms. Johnson. At least, not just yet.

🍎 *Baltimore Sun,* December, 1979.

*E*mbracing the New Lepers

> And His disciples asked Him, "Rabbi, who sinned, this man or his parents, that he was born blind?" Jesus answered, "It was not that this man sinned or his parents, but that the works of God might be made manifest in him."
>
> --John 9:2-3

We Americans have a strange way of making all serious diseases look like the Bubonic Plague. Now and then, when one finally happens along that really should remind us of the Black Death, our theological resources for dealing with it often seem more primitive than our limited medical abilities.

A few years ago, herpes was one of the major preoccupations in this country. *Time* and *Newsweek,* perhaps the best set of thermometers for taking the culture's collective temperature, added to the fever by serving up an abundant supply of lesions and apocalyptic sentiments about a disease that, in the grand scheme of things medical, turns out to be really quite unimportant. It is not surprising, then, that little more than faint rumblings were heard from conservative religious thinkers about the theological ramifications of herpes.

But AIDS appears to be another story. For one thing, unlike herpes it is usually fatal. It also seems, so far at least, to have afflicted primarily homosexuals and intravaneous drug abusers. The combination of these two facts has sparked in conservative religious thinkers around the country a very old answer -- retributive justice.

Lex talonis, the law of retribution, is a theological perspective deeply etched in the hearts of many people. I say "etched" because it seems to me to require a certain amount of hardening of the heart to remain loyal to this early Old Testament point of view. In Exodus, the plagues of Egypt were explained as just punishment for the sins of the pharaoh. Since that time, there seem always to have been enough well meaning but self-righteous individuals around to allow retributive justice to survive.

Now, the Rev. Jerry Falwell and others have applied the old formula to the victims of AIDS. It appears to fit quite nicely. They have done something wrong, and the hand of a righteous God is striking them down.

Ironically, in the Book of Job, an Old Testament work written centuries after Exodus, we find a sustained attack on retributive justice as a proper interpretation of the meaning of human suffering. Indeed, the omniscient narrator of Job is very careful in the opening verse of the first chapter to point out the protagonist is "blameless and upright."

Yet, Job suffers through a series of calamities rarely endured by any one man, save Voltaire's Candide or the victims described in Ivan Karamazov's tale. The only two things Job does not lose, in his long ordeal are life and his wife. And we must keep in mind it is his spouse who suggests, in the midst of Job's suffering, that he might think about cursing God and dropping dead.

Job's miseries are also not made any easier by the appearance of three friends who constantly berate him for having secretly done something to deserve his suffering. Through it all, however, Job steadfastly insists on his innocence. Although scholars continue to debate whether there is an answer to the problem of evil to be found in the Book of Job, all biblicists agree the old solution of deserved punishment is shown in the archaic tale to be intellectually and morally indefensible.

Conservative theologians don't much quote the Book of Job when discussing the victims of AIDS -- primarily because any distinctions found there between sinner and saved, chaff and wheat seem simplistic and inadequate. This points to a curious kind of theological sleight of hand that goes on in the thinking of the religious right. Biblical texts are only quoted when they serve their own narrow and self-interested interpretation. The text acts as a kind of theological ink-blot test, telling us more about the reader than what is on the page. Other texts that may contradict their point of view are frequently ignored. Those pericopes that show a theological sophistication that goes beyond *lex talonis* are made to disappear by some form of exegetical magic.

In our own time, Albert Camus in his novel, *The Plague,* appears also to have had a keen sense of the shortcomings of retributive justice as a mature and coherent response to the problem of suffering. In Camus' work, the North African town of Oran becomes inexplicably inundated by an outbreak of the Black Death. Father Paneloux, a Jesuit scholar and pastor of the local church, gives a sermon, complete with a theological explanation for the growing number of deaths:

"...Calamity has come on you, my brethren, and my brethren, you deserve it" -- there was a flutter of aghast surprise that extended to the crowd massed in the rain outside the porch. In strict logic what came next did not seem to follow from the dramatic opening. Only as the sermon proceeded did it become apparent to the congregation that, by a skillful oratorical device, Father Paneloux had launched at them, like a fisticuff, the gist of the whole discourse. After launching it he went on at once to quote a text from Exodus relating to the plague of Egypt, and said: "The first time this scourge appears in history, it was wielded to strike down the enemies of God. Pharaoh set himself up against the Divine will, and the plague beat him to his knees. Thus, from the dawn of recorded history, the scourge of God has humbled the proud of heart and laid low those who hardened themselves against Him. Ponder this well, my friends, and fall on your knees."

Later in *The Plague,* this sermon, which could have been torn from the homiletic notes of any of a number of contemporary television preachers, is shown to be an insufficient response to the reality of suffering experienced beyond the confines of the pulpit. The priest's transformation begins when he is called to the home of M. Othon. There Father Paneloux finds a tiny child in the throes of the last stages of the plague.

"...And just then, the boy had a sudden spasm, as if something had bitten him in the stomach, and uttered a long, shrill wail. For moments that seemed endless, he stayed in a queer, contorted position, his body racked by convulsive tremors; it was as if his frail frame were bending before the fierce breath of the plague, breaking under the reiterated gusts of fever..."

Through the confrontation with the child's physician, a man who had become intimately and practically involved with the plague sufferers, the priest comes to the realization of the absolute innocence of the boy. Later, he gives a second sermon in which he shifts from the use of the accusatory "you" to a more compassionate "we" in describing the possible victims of the plague. Indeed, he eventually assists in a practical way, in the alleviation of suffering by helping with medical treatments and in burying the dead.

Recently, while watching a broadcast of CBS's *60 Minutes,* I could not help but think of Camus' novel. One segment involved an interview with the first American family to contract AIDS. The father, a hemophiliac, received the disease through a blood transfusion. He unwittingly passed it on to his wife. The couple's baby, a frail little boy, contracted AIDS through the birth canal. It is clear these people have done nothing to warrant the suffering they now endure.

It is just as clear this disease will continue to attack more babies, and hemophiliacs, and drug abusers and homosexuals, and perhaps some of the rest of us, in the foreseeable future. It will not be made any easier for the victims by pointing an accusing finger in their direction.

A few weeks ago, while walking across campus on a sunlit fall afternoon, an older and much wiser colleague told me of a sermon she had heard the day before. It was given by a young priest, a man who divides his time between our campus and the shock trauma unit of a local hospital. For the last few years, he has had quite a bit of practical experience in formulating a theology of suffering. In his homily, he mentioned St. Francis' admonition to embrace the leper. We don't do much of that these days.

Newsday, November, 1985.

The Charles Curran Controversy

In the early days of the Second Vatican Council, Pope John XXIII, the architect of the changes in the Roman Catholic Church that took place in the early 1960's, remarked that he was in the process of opening the windows of the Church to allow in some fresh air.

Judging by the recent action of Cardinal Joseph Ratzinger, Prefect for the Congregation for the Doctrine of the Faith, to ban Father Charles Curran from teaching moral theology at the Catholic University of America, people both inside and outside the Roman Church might well ask if those windows have not once again been closed, with a resounding thud -- and perhaps locked as well.

Cardinal Ratzinger's decision, which required and received the approval of Pope John Paul II, was occasioned by Father Curran's books and scholarly articles, in which the moral theologian has suggested that Catholics should be free to use their consciences in regard to contraception, premarital sex and other moral issues.

The elements of the Curran case are, to say the least, quite complex. They are made even more so by a lack of basic agreement about the fundamental ground rules of the debate. Cardinal Ratzinger holds the position, as does the pope, that Catholic moral theologians cannot dissent from hierarchical Church teachings, even those that are non-infallible. Father Curran has repeatedly reaffirmed his belief in the Church's infallible teachings, but points out that the papacy has made no pronouncements, *ex cathedra,* and thus infallibly, about the sexual moral issues in question.

The Curran affair is made even murkier when one begins to understand that several theologians, particularly in Germany and Holland, hold similar if not identical views to those of

Father Curran on abortion, contraception, and homosexuality. But most of these men have never been called on the Vatican carpet. In a meeting with Cardinal Ratzinger on March 8, Father Curran pointed out this inequity. The cardinal responded by asking, "Well, Father, would you like to accuse these people? The Congregation will look into it."

A third factor that serves to confound the case of Father Curran is the realization that active Catholic parishioners generally reject the Church hierarchy's strong stance against contraception and divorce, and are far more divided on issues such as abortion and women serving as priests than the Church may understand or be willing to admit.

A recent survey conducted at the University of Notre Dame by David Leege and Monsignor Joseph Gremillion points out that the majority of Catholics surveyed disagreed with the statement: "The Church should remain strongly opposed to the use of contraceptives." Similar dissent was voiced by those Catholics when asked about the Church's position on divorce and remarriage.

Although the majority of Catholics studied in the Notre Dame survey are opposed to abortion, as well as women priests, the percentage of those in favor of limited abortion and female priests has doubled in the last ten years. One element that makes the Notre Dame study unique is that it concentrated on what it called committed "core Catholics," and did not include individuals who described themselves as marginal or lapsed Catholics.

Another issue that makes the firing of Charles Curran complicated and more than a little disconcerting is the realization that the Church's track record in censuring theologians, philosophers, biblical scholars, and sometimes even scientists, is not, even by conservative standards, always something to be admired. In 1610, Cardinal Robert Bellarmine was called before the Congregation for the Doctrine of the Faith, then called the Inquisition, for suggesting the distinction between the temporal and spiritual powers of the papacy. In the 20th century, all Western democracies hold this distinction to be immeasurably important and valuable.

In more recent times the eminent French Dominican, Marie-Joseph Lagrange, founder of the *Ecole Biblique* in Jerusalem and the prestigious *revue biblique* was subjected to bitter criticism by the Church hierarchy for a paper he delivered in Fribourg in 1897 on the sources of the Pentateuch, the first five books of the Old Testament. He was publicly criticized again in 1903 when he published his *la methode historique* a work that furthered the thesis he introduced at Fribourg. In 1907 Lagrange abandoned the study of the Old Testament in order to avoid more controversy. For the next few years he turned his scholarly interest to the New Testament. But in 1911, when Lagrange published his commentary on the gospel of Mark, the Church issued a Consistorial Decree, a disciplinary measure that led Lagrange to leave the *Ecole* a short time later.

In the years since Lagrange's difficulties with the authorities, history has declared the soft-spoken French Dominican the winner. Today Lagrange is rightfully associated with the revival early in this century of a then-moribund Catholic biblical scholarship. Indeed, Pope Pius XII's encyclical, *Divino Afflante Spiritu,* written in 1943, praises Lagrange's *Ecole Biblique* as one of the great centers of Catholic biblical scholarship.

The 20th century has also brought a range of decrees and censures of scholars that today should be a source of embarrassment for any thinking Catholic. In 1904 Father Henry Poels, a Dutch biblicist, raised doubts that the Pentateuch was written in its entirety by the hand of Moses. Some years before, the Pontifical Biblical Commission had ruled that Genesis through Deuteronomy were to be attributed to Moses. Despite the massive amount of evidence Poels collected to support his position, as well as his insistence that he was not tampering with any of the Church's infallible pronouncements, he was fired by the Catholic University.

Today, nearly all reputable Old Testament scholars, hold a view about the sources of the Pentateuch nearly identical in general outline to the position described by Poels before his firing in 1904.

In the 1880's another social reformer/priest, Edward McGlynn, was excommunicated for being a socialist. In 1892 McGlynn's case was reviewed. After a committee appointed by a papal representative suggested McGlynn's view of private property did not violate the position set out by Pope Leo XIII in his encyclical, *Rerum Novarum,* McGlynn was restored to his former position. In the years while he waited for his review, he lived and worked with New York City's poor. It is more than a little ironic that just three decades before the McGlynn case, when most Catholic moral theologians saw slavery as a profound moral evil, the Holy Office, under the direction of Pope Pius IX, issued a document suggesting that slavery was not, in fact, an "intrinsic" moral evil.

The Curran affair differs markedly from the cases of McGlynn, Poels and Lagrange, in that Father Curran has some options available that the others lacked. One way the moral theologian might proceed in an effort to regain his job is to appeal not just to the Congregation for Defense of the Faith, a bleak prospect at best, or to an academic committee of the university, but to a secular court. The number and range of legal issues such a case would call into play would be not only immense but also painful and embarrassing for Father Curran, for the university, and for the Church.

Given the spector of secular legal proceedings, the Church's history of dealing with dissent on non-infallible matters, its selective prosecution of Father Curran, as well as the Congregation's rather murky view of what counts as academic freedom, it might be more reasonable for the Congregation to reconsider a proposal made by Father Curran to Cardinal Ratzinger that the moral theologian should cease discussing matters pertaining to sexual ethics while still retaining his professorship.

It is a suggestion that might be taken seriously if the windows of the Church are still open. But from where many Catholics are standing these days, those windows look locked shut.

Baltimore Sunday Sun, September, 1986.

*F*aith, Ambiguity, and Wonder: *S*ome comments on Agnes of God

Drama, more than any of the other arts, has always been an exercise in the possible. *Agnes of God* is clearly one of those plays that reminds us of that fact. Through the craft of the play, we are opened up to possibilities. We are introduced to an ambiguity that produces possibilities: the tension between faith and reason, religion and science, the sacred and the profane. Even the names of the characters in this play are a kind of crafted ambiguity. Agnes, the young nun, takes her religious name from a third century Roman saint. When St. Agnes was 13 she consecrated her life to Jesus, declaring herself the bride of Christ. In a rage, her fiance's father, a Roman official, caused her to be brought to a brothel, where she was stripped of her garments. Later, the prefect said that she was to be burned at the stake, but she miraculously stood unharmed in the midst of the fire. Finally, one of the soldiers standing by was ordered to strike off her head with his sword. Needless to say, the number of parallels to the ancient Agnes are quite striking. The young nun of the play spends considerable time singing the *Agnus Dei,* "the lamb of God." Curiously enough, in French *Agnes* means something quite different. Cassell tells us it denotes a "simpleton, a raw young girl."

Mother Miriam Ruth's name is no less ambiguous. "Ruth" in Hebrew is usually identified with the noun "friend." In the Old Testament, Miriam was the woman responsible for saving the baby Moses from the bullrushes. The rabbis, however, have traditionally understood "Miriam" to be etymologically related to the word for "bitterness." In Arabic, *maram,* a possible cognate of Miriam, means "the wished for child."

The name Livingstone also contains some marvelous ambiguities. In the context of the New Testament "stones" are often referred to as object lessons. They are sterile in Mat. 3:9, dumb in Luke 19:40, but hard to swallow in Mat. 4:3 and 7:9. The good seed also falls on stony ground in Mat. 13:5, a ground that consists of a very shallow soil with stone near the top.

The etymological ambiguity is perhaps a key to much larger ambiguities within the play. The Doctor is pragmatic, efficient, dutiful to her patients. She stopped believing in God years before when her young sister, a nun, died because of carelessness and a lack of concern by her fellow nuns. Yet, at the same time, the psychiatrist is also a woman who, very early in the play, wishes out loud that atheists had a set of words that meant as much as "God love her" does to the believer. Similarly, Mother Miriam is an intelligent, perceptive, former chain smoker. There is a crafted ambiguity here. It would have been easier and less interesting if the Mother Superior were merely made an older version of Agnes. But she is not. She is not that simple.

Ambiguity. It teaches us something about the two world views that alternately clash and intermingle in this play. Most of us are serious people who have pressed hard for a reasoned world view. We have many reasons for rejecting traditional religious answers, but our nonreligious answers, like Livingstone's psychoanalysis, must also be subjected to the same kind of scrutiny. It too must meet the same criteria of consistency, clarity, and closeness to experience, and it has not unambiguously passed.

What one does with ambiguity is another lesson to be learned from the play. The psychoanalyst, through much of the play, denies the notion that the facts by their very nature are ambiguous. The Mother, on the other hand, is fully receptive to possibilities. She reminds us that "what we've gained in logic, we've lost in faith. We no longer have any sort of primitive wonder."

The play gives us a number of perspectives on the relationship of faith and wonder. For Mother Miriam, faith is an uninhibited willingness to make an assumption that divinity is present. There are also some rather different views of faith, most of which are variously offered by the Doctor. One is that it is a magical way of knowing things that can also be known by ordinary means; another is that piety involves believing something that is contrary to evidence; a third is that faith is being docile enough to be told what to believe instead of finding out for yourself. If Livingstone distrusts faith because she construes it in these ways, she does it for good reasons. Yet it is a pity if that leads her to deny the place that faith, properly understood, plays in life.

Mother Miriam, I think, is closer to the truth. Faith is something that is set in opposition to knowledge, not because it contradicts it, but because it exceeds knowledge where life gives occasion to exceed -- by feeling. And faith is a matter of feeling. It is a willingness to give way to feeling that all things flow together in a unity, a perfection, although we can't see it. It is a willingness to affirm perfection without waiting or asking for proof. It is a willingness to give actual things meaning by viewing them against an ideal background.

But faith also involves doubt, and doubt is often the ultimate tester. Faith, unless it is mere credulity, which does not deserve the name, is a series of encounters with doubt, it is perpetual little deaths and resurrections, it is cynicism met with transcendence, but never evaded. If faith has an enemy, it is not science, it is pretending to have faith. And pretending involves a lack of understanding -- understanding that the only way through doubt is the long way through indirection, through a faith that survives its own death daily.

Perhaps this doubt is what separates Mother Miriam from Sister Agnes. Doubt. For Agnes, it is not a possibility. Perhaps it is something feared, isolated, and for that reason made palpable. For Agnes, doubt is eliminated by indiscriminate assent. Everything is to be accepted. No doubts need apply. This assent leads to an odd kind of joy. Doubt is what also separates Mother Miriam from contemporary Jesus freaks. Their manic assent leads to a cultivated joy. They are often people who continually have to remind themselves how happy they are. Ironically, the Jesus they so uncritically accept is said to have wept in the garden, and cried out helplessly on the cross. And judging from these signs, Jesus was no Jesus freak.

Faith also has another component -- wonder. Wonder always begins with an element of surprise. The now obsolete "wonderstruck" suggests that wonder breaks into consciousness with a dramatic suddenness that produces amazement. To wonder is to perceive with reverence and love, and in wondering we come close to the feeling that the earth is holy. It used to be that the church or synagogue gave us the background for wonder, but now things have changed. One of the curious things about this play is it allows us to wonder.

Doctor Livingstone is reasonable. As Mother Miriam reminds us, she is also like most of us: "sensible people, feet on the ground, money in the bank, innocence trampled underfoot. Our minds dissected, our bodies cut open. 'No soul here, no heaven, no hell.' Well, we're better off. Less disease for one thing. No room for miracles." We all miss the miracles, for we are, unfortunately, more like the Doctor than the Mother Superior. But it is curious that in the theater we come closer to praying than many of us have in a long time. We open up the possibility to wonder.

Not long ago the playwright, John Pielmeier, remarked that a psychiatrist who had been invited to read the play had commented that the only mistake of Doctor Livingstone was that she was a bad psychiatrist. She became obsessed with her patient. Perhaps the real psychiatrist was correct. But this is not Doctor Livingstone's only problem. Through most of the play she has an inability to nurture openness and epistemelogical humility in the face of the possibility of mystery. She falls into a kind of psychoanalytic idolatry whose myths, symbols and theories are often inadequate and crude efforts to domesticate a reality that often eludes explanation. It is doubtful God died the day the Doctor ceased to believe in a personal deity, but she very well may have begun to die herself on the day her life ceased to be illuminated by the steady radiance, renewed intermittently, of a wonder, the source of which is perhaps beyond all reason.

Commentar, Spring 1980.

"Nobody Left in School"

The time: late October, 1986.
The place: Hawkins County, Tenn.

Mrs. Bunpenny, the office secretary for the South Hawkins County High School, enters the principal's private office.

Mrs. B.P.:	*Excuse me Mr. Peters, you have some people waiting to see you.*
Principal Peters:	*Mrs. Bunpenny, I told you not to bother me with students. I didn't spend all those years in the classroom with those hoodlums only to be bothered by them now that I'm principal. Tell them to see the vice-principal.*
B.P.:	*But Mr. Peters, they aren't students, they're parents.*
P.P.:	*Well...in that case (he straightens his tie and examines the part in his hair by checking his reflection in the Junior Chamber of Commerce award hanging on the wall behind his desk) have them come in right away.*
B.P.:	*All of them, sir?*
P.P.:	*What do you mean, "All of them"?*
B.P.:	*There are quite a few of them, sir. In fact, the line stretches all the way around the building and across to the Fighting Hawks' football field.*
P.P.:	*(He moves to the window.) What are they all doing out there?*
B.P.:	*They are waiting to see you, sir.*

P.P.: *I know that, Mrs. Bunpenny. But why do they want to talk to me?*

B.P.: *From what I can gather, Mr. Platon, he's from the Flat Earth Society, we have his boy, Bill, in the junior class, it seems he's a little upset about what's going on in his son's physics class. He said he'd like to teach his son physics at home.*

P.P.: *That's the most ridiculous thing I have ever heard. Give him detention.*

B.P.: *Principal Peters, you can't give Mr. Platon detention, he's not a student here.*

P.P.: *Then give his kid detention and tell the father I'm too busy to talk to him.*

B.P.: *What should I do with the others, sir?*

P.P.: *(Looking furtively through the venetian blinds.) Who else is out there?*

B.P.: *Some Hindu parents complaining about hamburgers served in the school cafeteria, some Moslems upset about the hot dogs, a few Hasidic Jews who don't want their sons traveling with girls on the school bus, a couple of Mormons who object to parts of our American history class, and some ladies who are upset because we're still reading* Macbeth *in senior English.*

P.P.: *What's wrong with* Macbeth *this time?*

B.P.: *It's the ghosts again, sir.*

P.P.: *I thought we took the ghosts out because they were violating someone's constitutional rights.*

B.P.: *We did. But these parents are from the Casper the Friendly Ghost Church of the Holiness. They think we should put the ghosts back in.*

P.P.: *Well...ah...tell them I'm not here. Tell them to go see the vice-principal.*

B.P.: *What should I do about the Ba'hai couple?*

P.P.: *The what couple?*

B.P.: *The Ba'hai couple, they're very angry about what we did to Anne Frank.*

P.P.: *Mrs. Bunpenny, you know I can't keep track of what happens to every single student in this school. What class is she in?*

B.P.: *Who?*

P.P.: *Anne Frank.*

B.P.: *It's a book, sir. Remember....? You had to take it out of the curriculum because it was offensive to their religious beliefs.*

P.P.: *Oh...right...right, that was the part when Anne suggested all the religions are equal. Well, we stopped reading it, didn't we?*

B.P.: *Yes sir, but you've got some hopping mad Ba'hais outside because they believe all religions are equal.*

P.P.: *What do they expect me to do?*

B.P.: *They want you to put Anne Frank back in the classroom. They are walking around with "Free Anne Frank" buttons and the Friends of* The Wizard of Oz *aren't happy about it because the Ba'hais are butting up in line.*

P.P.: *Tell them all to take their children home for whatever classes they find objectable. That's what the federal judge said, didn't he?*

(Mrs. Bunpenny exits. A few minutes later, Principal Peters looks out the window to discover the line of unruly parents has completely disappeared. He wears the look of satisfaction when his secretary reenters.)

P.P.: *Well, Mrs. Bunpenny, I guess we took care of that. It's clear all we need around here is some good, incisive decision-making.*

B.P.: *There's just one more problem, sir. There's a line of teachers waiting outside to see you.*

P.P.: *What's their problem?*

B.P.: *They want to know if they can go home early. It seems everyone else did.*

      🍎 Baltimore Evening Sun, November, 1986.

Note: In October of 1986, several books, including *The Wizard of Oz, Alice in Wonderland, The Diary of Anne Frank,* and *Macbeth,* were removed from the Tennessee public school reading list by a federal judge in that state because those books violated the constitutional rights of students who were members of certain conservative Christian sects.

DEATH

In the last analysis it is our conception of death which decides the answers to all the questions life puts to us.

-- Dag Hammarskjold

The Cold Breath of Dachau

There have been few moments in my life I would call truly revelatory. When these experiences occur, it is like someone or something holds me in its grip, forcing me to pay careful attention to signs that must be read. On each of these occasions, it is as if the hands of the Divine have driven an imaginary stake through my shoes so I may not move from that spot until the revelation is complete.

Usually these brief theophanies involve an understanding of the goodness of things, the essential sacredness of life. At other times, such revelations involve the apprehension of a much more malevolent, darker side of life. On still even rarer occasions, I am reminded of both.

Recently, while reading of the controversy surrounding President Reagan's plans to visit the West German cemetery at Bitburg, I learned with great interest that the president will pass by the site of the former Nazi concentration camp at Dachau, though he apparently will not stop there. I found this information interesting because it was at Dachau, on a bitterly cold January day in 1979, I had one of those rare revelatory experiences.

The morning of that day had broken clear and cold. For several hours we had driven through the Bavarian countryside, admiring snow-covered hills that gently rise from the Amper River which was then partially frozen and dotted with ice skaters. On the summit of one of those hills stands the mid-16th century castle of Wittelsbacher and, beyond it, the industrial town of Dachau.

The concentration camp, erected on the site of an old World War I munitions factory, is situated a little more than a mile from the early 17th century town hall and the parish church built in 1625. Although the camp is a 15-minute walk from the center of town, it was difficult to find anyone willing or able to give directions.

The buildings in the mile-square camp have been leveled. All that remains are the cracked concrete foundations of structures that housed 230,000 kidnapped souls from 1933 to 1945. The rectangular barracks were set out in a precise grid-like arrangement. The only differences between one building and the next were the terrors and nightmares they contained.

Now, 35 years later, I stopped with my German companion, a young physician, at the intersection of two of those rows of vanished buildings. At the far end I could see an aluminum sculpture erected in the 1960's and dedicated to the memory of thousands of human beings who forfeited their lives in that camp.

The metal structure is fashioned in the shape of a tree, but the limbs and branches, upon closer look, more clearly resemble the anguished and contorted bodies of the victims of the Holocaust. Most of the faces of these figures are twisted in grotesque and silent screams.

As I stood at the cross roads of that camp the feeling of being inexplicably riveted to that spot overtook me. I knew I could not move. I also knew I was to learn something important there, something I was not to forget.

A few moments later, a chilling wind began to blow from the direction of the sculpture. It was an eerie gust, not made of one substance. It was more like the breaths of thousands of anonymous sufferers wedded in one bone-chilling, collective wail.

In another moment, I was certain my frozen ears would fall from my face. I have not felt that mysterious numbing cold before or since. In an instant, however, the gale abruptly abated as enigmatically as it had begun. But the memory of that wind, which sounded more like the steady wail of anguished human voices, still remains.

When I learned of Mr. Reagan's plans to by-pass Dachau on his way to Bitburg, I remembered the story the president told to three Jewish dignitaries visiting the White House last year. In that meeting, as his guests remembered it, the president told of serving with a film crew which accompanied the allied troops who entered the concentration camp in 1945.

Later, Reagan's aides apologized for the error: the president was misunderstood. He had not gone to Germany at the end of the war. But all three visitors understood him to have said just that.

After visiting Dachau in 1979, I will never be confused about whether I was there. It would be much more difficult to forget if I were there in 1945, or any of the 12 years before. It is a pity Mr. Reagan will not stop at Dachau. If he did, he could learn, even today, why he should not go to Bitburg.

Baltimore Evening Sun, May, 1985.

Death on the Coffee Table

To Live Until We Say Good-Bye is another book about death. As you may know, there have been quite a few of those lately. This one is special, it might be argued, for it's written by Elisabeth Kubler-Ross -- the one woman army against the Grim Reaper. Although it's the type of book one is supposed to like -- glossy pictures of dying people, interspersed with thanatological gems by Kubler-Ross -- it nevertheless had the same effect on me that Chinese food often does -- filling me up very quickly, only to leave me empty a few hours later.

The book consists of three separate photo-essays about former patients of Kubler-Ross: the first a 42-year-old former actress dying of abdominal cancer; the second, a child of five, suffering with an inoperable brain tumor; the last a 57-year-old social worker who has decided against radiation or surgery in her struggle with breast cancer. With the varied social-economic backgrounds, ages, and types of disease, one would expect that each of the three would have her own story to tell. Unfortunately, this expectation became my greatest disappointment with the book. Kubler-Ross manages to tell us very little about the three patients and instead demonstrates how frightfully easy it is, even for a good therapist, to go looking for elements in patients that reaffirm her own attitude toward death. In doing this she has ignored some differences that may show us that there are as many "death styles" as there are "life styles."

In the beginning of *To Live Until We Say Good-Bye* Kubler-Ross tells us "...it is the purpose of this book to show what can and will happen to human beings, young and old, child and adult alike, when they are in the process of being destroyed by a malignant growth and yet can emerge as a butterfly emerges from a cocoon with a sense of peace and freedom, not only in themselves, but in those who have the courage to say good-bye, knowing that every good-bye also includes a hello."

It is clear, for Kubler-Ross at least, the "hello" occurs in the afterlife. Indeed, the two women, as well as the mother of the little girl, are all quite emphatic that there is a life beyond. Although I don't have a quarrel with eternity, I do wonder why all the "adjusted" patients we meet in Kubler-Ross's books always seem to mirror her attitude toward death. Because she is a Jungian therapist, she cannot conceive of the possibility that her patients might not share her enthusiasm for the prospects of immortality, or that there could be substantial numbers of "healthy" people who fear death.

I am disturbed by the dust jacket almost as much as the book. In no uncertain terms we are told: *To Live Until We Say Good-Bye* is a landmark book that shows Kubler-Ross's counselling work with terminally ill patients as she brings them to acceptance of death."

It may be symptomatic of an age when fear and guilt are no longer existential categories, but, rather, minor annoyances to be disposed of like the garbage or an uninvited guest. Kubler-Ross has emerged as the high-priestess of death in an era of self-help books -- an era when we almost have ourselves believing that since I'm O.K. and you're O.K., death is fine, too. We now travel to death seminars, join thanatology sensitivity groups, and buy "death with dignity" t-shirts. La Rochefoucauld believed that thinking about death was like staring at the sun. I only wonder if we aren't doing what many of us did as children during a solar eclipse -- we look over our shoulder at a shadow made by a pinhole, while applauding one another for "dealing" with it.

The City Paper, November, 1978.

A Sister Died

One of our sisters here at Notre Dame has died. She was a good woman, but by no means remarkable, save her omnipresent kindness. For over four decades she taught and made art as a School Sister of Notre Dame in many different settings that included a half a dozen grade schools, as well as this proud college on North Charles Street. The most lasting memory I will most likely carry away from her funeral is how quickly she managed to learn the names of new faculty members, often to the embarrassment of the newcomers. Luckily, they could feign reciprocation by using the generic "sister" -- a ubiquitous and entirely appropriate description whose truth required no first or last name accompany it.

It is curious that a decade or so ago the organizers and participants of the then-burgeoning women's movement chose the word "sister" to designate their compatriots. It is significant that these quiet and confident women of Notre Dame had been calling each other "sister" a century before as they literally built this place from the ground up, brick by painful brick. They did it without men then, and, with the exception of a handful of male faculty members, and a larger number of female instructors, they are still doing it that way today.

Sister John Bersch was not alone in her dying; a 24-hour-a-day vigil was kept at her bedside by the women with whom she had taught all these years. Nearly all of her sisters took a turn: There is the octogenarian biology teacher who recently celebrated her birthday by going to the classroom as usual. Her students marked the occasion, however, by taking out an ad in the school paper wishing her a happy birthday; There is the slender and angular poet -- a woman who regularly manages to construct delicate poems full of power and grace. This extraordinary woman once told me of the years of teaching summer school and receiving $5 each August in the form of a mass offering for the entire summer's labors. Now she listens attentively as I tell her what I am writing these days. She never bothers to cloud the conversation with her accomplishments.

There is also the senior member of my department, a 65-year-old dynamo, who last fall asked me if I could recommend her for a sabbatical, her first in 43 years of teaching. It wasn't because she was tired. She needed to attend important chapter meetings in Rome.

These women, and many others, helped Sister John go gentle into that good night -- all realizing that in the final analysis faith is a walking to the edge of all the light there is and then taking one more step.

Ironically enough, in the time since the beginning of the women's movement, nuns have become fair game. We have seen in the last several years the emergence of a rash of films and plays all with the seeming intent of externalizing our worst information and prejudices about these quiet and powerful sisters. But daily contact with these women teaches one that they are, if nothing else, very complex. They are stylish and sometimes not so sartorially sophisticated, they are brilliant, but more often ordinary, they are staunchly conservative, but just as frequently fiercely liberal. Working with these sisters, one is ultimately forced to abandon all of the cliches in an attempt at the telling of these complicated lives.

Outside in what is erroneously called "the real world" by those who still carry in their heads images of flying nuns and sanguine, Dominique-singing penguins on the Ed Sullivan Show, the dying is not nearly so easy, and so we have a culture of books to show us how. There are now so many of these tracts any bookstore can be found to contain two or three shelves devoted to what is called "thanatology." These usually can be found next to *How to Be Your Own Best Friend,* and *Looking Out for Number One.* We now learn to die in stages, our souls like some sort of metaphysical rockets shot from an earthly launching pad with little belief in any ultimate destination.

Meanwhile, back at Notre Dame, these gentle and strong women practice the ancient virtues of faith and charity, and, with pain and tears, they commit their sister to the ground, with a profound and mysterious hope that one day she will resurrect.

🍎 *Baltimore Evening Sun,* February, 1983.

The Frank Coppola Case

Shortly after 11:00 p.m. on August 10, Frank J. Coppola, convicted of the 1978 slaying of Murial Hatchell, a Newport News resident, became the fifth person in the United States since 1976, and the first individual in Virginia in over 20 years, to be executed by the state. Mr. Coppola's death was viewed by six unidentified civilian witnesses, the warden of Mecklenburg state prison, a state appointed physician, and, of course, the unidentified executioner.

There are several facets of this case that make it noteworthy. One of the most important of these is an unprecedented move made by Virginia Governor Charles Robb in which he ordered an immediate appeal of U.S. Court of Appeals Judge John Butzner's late stay of execution that would have allowed for a review of the constitutionality of the Virginia death penalty statute. As an editorial in the August 12 *Baltimore Sun* remarked "This led to the sorry spectacle of Virginia officials flying through the dusk to Washington urging the Supreme Court to overturn the appellate judge, the justices conferring by telephone under an eleventh hour deadline in a ugly parody of judicious deliberation, the death warrant approved by a five to three margin, and then, minutes later, the first jolt of electricity through Coppola's body." It was clear that the State of Virginia wished to execute Mr. Coppola, and that execution came despite a separate test of the constitutionality of the Virginia law that is still pending before the Supreme Court.

It is not just the infrequency of executions in this country, nor the vindictive move by Governor Robb, that makes the death of Mr. Coppola deserving of notice, it is also that he, like Gary Gilmore, the Utah man killed by firing squad in 1977, welcomed his punishment. Several months ago, after vigorously pursuing four years of appeals, Mr. Coppola stopped his petitioning. Subsequent appeals, including the one made to the Fourth U.S. Circuit Court of Appeals, were made by J. Gray

Lawrence, one of Coppola's former attorneys. His decision to forego any further appeals was motivated, Mr. Coppola said, by the desire to preserve his "dignity," as well as a wish to spare his family any more emotional turmoil. What makes Mr. Coppola's surrender to the dictum of the state most confusing is his insistence of innocence, voiced frequently during his early appeal process, and as late as the day of his execution. The jury, however, found overwhelming evidence to convict the former seminarian and policeman.

But perhaps the real significance of the Coppola case is that it once again gives us the opportunity to reevaluate our position on capital punishment. For some, Mr. Coppola's execution will be seen as a necessary corrective for a society whose members are seen as increasingly more vulnerable to violent crimes. For others, it is a distasteful reminder that our collective national attitude toward the use of the death penalty has become in recent years more vengeful, and, in the process, more irrational.

For those Americans who articulate their reasons for advocating capital punishment the most frequently advanced and widely accepted argument is that the fear of death deters people from committing crimes. In the United States, this has become an old saw, a bit of wisdom handed down from generation to generation. Unfortunately, it is not true. In this country the homicide rate since the mid-1950's has remained roughly constant, while the number of executions has decreased dramatically.

If the death penalty were a deterrent, states without it should have a significantly higher murder rate than states of similar socioeconomic makeup retaining it. Statistics from nearly all modern studies of capital punishment show this is not the case. In fact, in this country some states with the lowest murder rates have not had death penalty statutes for over one hundred years.

The abolitionist state of Wisconsin, for example, over a five year period had an annual homicide rate of 1.5 per 100,000 population. Neighboring Illinois, a capital punishment state, had a corresponding rate of 4.4 per 100,000. In a study of policemen murdered over a 25 year period in 11 death penalty states and six abolitionist states, Dr. Thorsten Sellin found that the murder rate in the death penalty states was 1.3 per 100,000, while it was 1.2 in states without capital punishment. Similar conclusions have been made using data culled from other states by Jake Gibbs in his *Crimes, Punishment and Deterrence* and Hans Zeisel's in his article, "The Deterrent Effect of the Death Penalty," written in 1977 for the *Supreme Court Review*.

From a historical point of view, if the existence of the death penalty had been the demonstrative deterrent we have been led to believe, the 18th century reign of the Hanover monarchs should have produced a Britain free of capital offenses. At that time, English Common Law included 350 crimes punishable by death. But as Dr. Samuel Johnson observed during this period: "The surest place to find most of London's pickpockets plying their trade is in a crowd assembled to witness one of their own being hung."

During a conversation with Judge Butzner, Mr. Coppola made his feelings known about the deterrence value of his death sentence: "I don't look at death that way. I don't fear death. I mean, that's no macho image or anything; that's my personal beliefs. Whatever anybody else feels, that's fine. The particular aspect of sitting in the chair and being electrocuted until I'm dead does not harbor any great fear for me." Historical as well as contemporary evidence points to the conclusion made by Professor Sellin in his *Death Penalty,* published by the American Law Institute, "Anyone who carefully examines the data is bound to arrive at the conclusion that the death penalty exercises no influences on the extent of fluctuating rates of capital punishment. It has failed as a deterrent."

Stripped of any real evidence for the deterrence value of the death penalty, the honest proponent of capital punishment is left with the other supposedly forceful argument. Most people are in favor of the death penalty because the criminal has perpetrated a horrible crime and only his execution will satisfy the injustice done and right the moral imbalance in the universe. This retributivist view has some interesting historical underpinnings. The death penalty was most probably initiated in ancient cultures as a purification rite, a cleansing of society contaminated by the criminal act. In order to placate the gods, and restore moral harmony, the perpetrator, or some suitable replacement, was sacrificed. It was only later in human history, after each member of the group began to be seen as an individual moral agent, that the idea of individual retribution came into being. The original desire to restore moral equilibrium, however, seems always to have been the strongest motivating factor in these early cultures. In a curious kind of way, we may well be witnessing the return of a cultural exorcising in the modern practice of capital punishment. This may say as much about the dark side of each of us as it does about the heinousness of our criminals. What vociferous Christian advocates of the death penalty who often quote the Deuteronomic "eye for an eye" fail to admit is that "turning the other cheek" and "forgiving our enemies 70 times seven" are also later parts of that revelatory Biblical ethic. Somehow these passages get lost, as a selective use of scripture for these people serves as a substitute for an honest and reasonable evaluation of the issue. Minds already made up search for proof texts to bolster their prejudices, while ignoring the first four centuries of Christian history -- centuries characterized by a zealous adherence to pacifism. What can be said about capital punishment as a means to retributive justice, as a way of restoring moral harmony in the universe, is that is has taken as the subjects of its legalized killing a disproportionate number of males, blacks, the poor, and pleaders of unpopular causes. "I have never seen a person of means go to the chair," wrote former Ohio governor, Michael DiSalle. "It is the have-nots who become society's blood sacrifice."

Since 1930 we have executed 3,863 people in the United States. 2,066 were black, 3,831 were men. Of the 455 persons convicted of rape and executed during that same period, 405 were black, all but two of those in the southern states. A careful, well-reasoned approach to these figures should lead us to a conclusion similar to Justice Douglas's concurring opinion in Furman vs. Georgia, where he cited with approval the definitive study, *The President's Commission on Law Enforcement:* "Finally, there is evidence that the imposition of the death sentence and the exercise of dispensing power by the courts and the Executive follow discriminatory patterns. The death penalty is disproportionately imposed and carried out on the poor, the negro, and the members of unpopular causes."

All five individuals executed since that landmark 1972 ruling have been white, but it is of some interest to note they have also all been males. The imposition of capital punishment may be one of the few times women should not object to being put on a pedestal, particularly if the alternative is being put in the chair.

The historical roots of the discriminatory use of the death penalty are sunk very deeply in Anglo-American culture. As late as 1819, English Common Law still provided the death penalty for 220 crimes, including shoplifting. Although the laws were not strictly enforced, courts handed down between 2,000 and 3,000 death sentences a year between 1805-1810 in Britain. Around 1810, however, the severity of the law began to be mitigated in the English Courts by several factors. Judges began arbitrarily to fix the value of stolen goods below the capital level. This was often linked with a second loop-hole, benefit of clergy, which was liberally interpreted to mean anyone who could read and write. The effect of these two practices, as well as a third, the acquisition of Royal pardons for those who could afford them, was the elimination of capital punishment for the educated and the rich. The first two of these practices were not uncommon in colonial America. If one adds to this notion that adequate legal defense could only be afforded by the wealthy, we have a formula that virtually guaranteed the execution of a disproportionate number of blacks and the poor in this country. Whether newly drafted capital punishment statutes will avoid these discriminatory practices remains to be seen. Many critics think they will not.

Although some may still believe that capital punishment restores the balance of moral order in the universe, a sober evaluation of the way the death penalty has been practiced in this country reveals that we rarely avenge the capital crimes of wealthy whites and women of any race. There is little reason to believe this will be different in the future.

The Coppola execution affords us the painful opportunity to reevaluate our points of view on capital punishment. Most of us will not take this opportunity. Instead, we will rely on emotions, passions, and faulty rhetoric which has been posing for wisdom in our culture for quite some time now.

❦   Unpublished, August, 1982.

One Last Mad and Decisive Act

The story of the Reverend Jim Jones and the Peoples Temple is a very strange, confusing and tragic one. It is, perhaps, made even more complex by knowing something of Jones and his movement.

In the 1950's, Jones was a young Congregational minister with a small church in Indianapolis. He lived simply, organized soup kitchens, built nursing homes and had tremendous appeal with minorities. As his following grew, Jones eventually withdrew from the Congregationalists, founding his own temple in a converted synagogue in Indianapolis.

In the mid-60's, his congregation, now approximately 80 percent black, continued to grow, often reaching out to people on the fringes of American society: transients, drug addicts and prostitutes. In return for a warm place to stay and a bite to eat, they became Jones' audience for lectures on the ills of the social and economic system and the dangers of racism.

By the late 1960's, as the group began to move politically to the left, it also moved theologically to the right. The religious content of Jones' message at this time became fundamentalist, born-again Christianity. He quoted liberally from the Bible and at the same time began to see Jesus as a divine social activist. He stressed the need for economic reform, but fused it with a good bit of that old-time religion. By 1969, with mounting pressure from Indianapolis authorities, Jones convinced approximately 70 families to move to Ukiah, in northern California, where he set up the Peoples Temple.

His sermons at the time were often a mixture of exhortation to brotherhood and equality, combined with often near-hysterical ranting about the inevitability of race wars. By the time the group had moved its headquarters to California, Jones had come to see himself as a reincarnation of Jesus and Karl Marx, often claiming that he had the ability to read minds and heal the sick. A few years later, after moving the Temple headquarters from Ukiah to San Francisco, he managed to get himself appointed the director of public housing for the city of San Francisco. The same personal magnetism and intelligence that helped him convince people to sell their homes and move with him to California also helped him gain some substantial influence in local politics.

Not long after this appointment as housing director, he began to feel that a number of high-ranking officials had a vendetta against him. In 1973, he started negotiations with the government of Guyana with the intention of establishing a religious settlement there. Construction of the settlement began in 1974 and in 1976 Jones and about 1,000 of the Temple's followers moved to what the former Congregationalist minister suggested they call "Jonestown."

A short time later, numerous complaints began to surface about brutal beatings, forced labor and people being held at gun point in Jonestown. In a two-year period between 1976 and 1978, over 1,200 letters were written to the State Department by friends of people living in the Jonestown community. Most of these charges were dismissed by the government as exaggeration. But after Representative Leo Ryan and several members of his fact-finding group were killed, it was apparent to the State Department, and to the rest of us, that Jonestown was no ordinary utopian agricultural movement.

In his last months Jones had become increasingly obsessed with the idea that America was out to get him. On numerous occasions he preached four-hour long sermons, broadcast on the loudspeaker system, in which he extolled the virtues of the movement and warned against the encroachment of the CIA and other organizations.

Jones also began to hold rehearsals for mass suicides. These practice sessions were called "white nights," and toward the end they occurred as frequently as several times a week. The purpose of these rehearsals, in part, seemed to be both a testing of members to see if they were loyal enough to die for the movement, and the rehearsal of a contingency plan in case of what Jones foresaw as an "attack."

It is very difficult to explain why over 900 people took their lives in Guyana. The life of Jones, however, certainly suggests an ability to move people in a way that is beyond the ordinary. If we consider he continually displayed a kind of power and charisma that convinced people to do a number of things that went against their best interest, we may have at least one small key to what went on in Jonestown. There is, of course, the very real possibility many people chose the poison over being gunned down by Jones' loyalists. Stanly Clayton, a survivor of the ordeal, described to reporters how a number of residents were forced into taking the poison while Jones stood screaming, "Be quiet and die with dignity. Hurry up." Still, it is also apparent that the larger number of people drank the Kool-aid and cyanide quite voluntarily. Odell Rhodes, another survivor who escaped by hiding in the jungle, claims that although most of the children and a number of the adults had to be coerced into taking the poison, the majority of members took it willingly while the leader reassured them that they would "all meet again in the after-life."

In the last several months, the Jonestown founder had become increasingly out of touch with reality. He may have interpreted the arrival of Congressman Ryan as a threat to the very survival of the movement and the members themselves. Most authorities on suicide constantly stress that one of the basic preludes to suicide is the experience of an overwhelming loss and an accompanying feeling of impotence. In ill health and full of grief and fear over the destruction of a community he saw as idyllic, Jones transformed those feelings into a kind of martyrdom rewarded by the guarantee of a life beyond.

In a somewhat similar situation, all the members of a fortress west of the Dead Sea, Masada, in 74 A.D., together with women and children, chose death over captivity. Over 900 members of the community at Masada, which was the last stronghold of the zealots, a radical Jewish group of the day, committed suicide rather than submit to the Roman legions of Titus. The ancient historian, Josephus, relates that the commander at Masada, Eleazer, reminded his troops of their original resolve never to become slaves to the Romans. He called on them to die by their own hands. When they hesitated, he added another argument -- that "death affords our souls their liberty and sends them to their own place of purity." His soldiers responded by killing their wives and children, some finally committing suicide and others drawing lots to determine who would kill his companions and then himself. When the Romans finally arrived at the fortress, the only people alive were two women and five children who had hidden in a cave and escaped massacre.

With Jim Jones becoming increasingly more convinced about the possibility of CIA invasion and political plots, his people may well have been galvanized to a psychological view not unlike the people of Masada. Although in the Judeo-Christian tradition we now tend to view the events of Masada through a long-angle lens, and hence, tend to evaluate the behavior there as morally admirable, I'm not so sure from a purely psychological standpoint that the two incidents are that different. The residents of Jonestown may have seen Mr. Ryan as a symbol of an overpowering America ready to destroy their community.

Emile Durkheim, the noted French sociologist, in his book, *Suicide,* declares that there are a number of distinctive kinds of suicides. One particular variety, which he called "altruistic suicide," usually occurs as the result of fanatical service to a group or ideal. In these cases the pressures of a social group are often so strong that individual identity is lost and self-destruction is demanded by the group, for a higher cause.

It is clear that in Jonestown, the image of Jim Jones had been blown up larger than life. He was a very vain man who fed on the adulation of his followers. The people were dependent on him and drew protection, power and a sense of belonging from him. It was certainly a surrender to his superior power that brought many of them to Guyana to begin with, and it may have been responsible for their deaths as well. Freud argued, in *Group Psychology and Analysis of the Ego,* that in the presence of an overpowering and charismatic figure, adults often behave as children, blindly following the voice of this new parental figure. They abandon their egos to his, identifying with his power. In Jonestown, Guyana on a mid-November day the power of that figure began to wane, and in one last mad and decisive act, he took his followers with him.

🍒 *Baltimore Sun,* November, 1978.

Scrooge and Marley: Partners in Death

Charles Dickens is dead. He died in June of 1870 following an afternoon of writing. Many people these days argue his books are dead, too. The Victorians, these critics inform us, were notoriously sentimental. They liked to shed tears. They showed emotions openly and often complimented each other for being "tender hearted." The heart, in fact, was a favorite symbol in the late 19th century whether it was on the frontispiece of a volume of poetry or embroidered on a sampler.

Some say Dickens's fiction is dead because, unlike the Victorians, we are not "soft hearted," we distrust emotions openly displayed. Those who do it are given over to "hearts and flowers," and this makes us unable to view Scrooge and Marley as anything but a quaint time piece written by a dead man about a dead past.

All of this would seem fairly reasonable except that the people who seem to enjoy the novel most are children. Children, of course, are farther from being dead than most of us. Perhaps children appreciate the book so much because they possess the required hopefulness and simplicity necessary to fully understand Christmas. But this essay is not just about mistletoe, good cheer and Christmas pudding. It is about being dead. In order to comprehend this we must understand the mind of Scrooge.

Scrooge undergoes a transformation, a conversion if you will. But it is not just the transformation of Scrooge. As Johnson points out in his excellent essay on the novel: "Scrooge's transformation is more than the conversion of a single human being. It is the plea for society to undergo a transformation." The dead Dickens is urging us to have "a change of heart."

This is not the first time Dickens has been concerned with the idea of conversion. Nancy attempts to convert Sikes; Oliver tries to transform Fagin. All of these transformations tell us a good deal about Dickens's view of human nature. His view of life was essentially hopeful. Dickens was a victim of poverty himself, the son of an imprisoned debtor. Later as a young newspaper reporter, he daily experienced the worst slums of London. He was intimately familiar with the various forms of human corruption and decay, but in spite of all this, Dickens believed that life, no matter how miserable or close to death, was not hopeless.

But the change of heart in this novel is not just a plea for an end to socio-economic inequities. It is certainly nothing as simple as Marx's revision of labor, it is a new theory of human value. Scrooge's conversion is a movement from frigidity to warmth, from isolation to community, from deadness to life.

It is significant that Scrooge never painted out Marley's name on the office door. There it stood for years: Scrooge and Marley. The two men are parts of a whole. Marley is a dead dead man. Scrooge is a living dead man. The dead Marley becomes a dead door knocker and in doing so shows Scrooge that the dead side of him needs to be resurrected.

Early in the novel, Scrooge believes that life in others, in Bob Cratchit, in Cratchit's family, and in his nephew, is humbug -- sentimentality if you like. Marley, of course, has only begun to understand his deadness in life after his deadness in death, and thus he must wear the chains his deadness in life has forged.

A Christmas Carol presents us with a series of chain and door images. Scrooge constantly tries to chain people to their work or lock them out of his office. The result, of course, is that he becomes chained and locked up in his living deadness. Eventually Scrooge becomes unbound and open through the aid of the three personified time elements, the past, the present and the future. These temporal figures help him to see his deadness in life by showing Scrooge his inability to remember the past, to understand the present, or to imagine the future, three signs of being dead. It is curious that the dead Dickens, a pre-Freudian sentimentalist, has Scrooge transported back to his childhood. In fact, the old man's movement back to life begins with the compassion he shows for the figure who was himself as a child. It is only through self-compassion and self-forgiveness that Scrooge begins to move outside the trap of his own consciousness and his living death. The roles of Marley and the Christmas Spirits are specifically therapeutic. They never tell Scrooge what to do, they allow him to see what he has been, what he is now, and the deadly future to which he was moving.

By the end of the novel, Scrooge begins to act like a child. Perhaps it is because he is sentimental, but it may also be because he is now alive with the kind of vitality possessed by a child. In a sense, he has taken the place of Tiny Tim. The conversion is complete, Scrooge now understands the importance of Christmas. Finally, Dickens leaves us with the notion that it may take just this kind of vitality and simplicity to comprehend why we come together in the dead of winter to read aloud a dead book about a dead man bringing a living dead man back to life.

Commentar, Winter 1979.

Dancing With Death

One main reason why traditional drama continues to have value for us is that it presents to us in its own way something that we meet in another form in nature or in our own lives. Michael Cristofer's *Shadow Box* is a significant play, among other reasons, because it presents us with, or rather puts us in touch with, three people who are dying. In the plotting of the play, Cristofer has skillfully woven together three variations on this important theme. The theme, of course, is the ultimate in existential paradoxes. It is the condition of infinity housed in finiteness. We as humans have a symbolic identity that brings us sharply out of nature. We have creative abilities that allow us to run intellectual rings around the other animals. We can sit comfortably in our living rooms and comtemplate the stars. Yet this infinite capacity is housed in a body that breathes, walks, feels pain, and eventually wears out, all too often at precisely the point when our lives show promise. It is a terrifying paradox with which to live. One that we'd rather not think about until it is thrust upon us.

Although the theme is the same, the responses to mortality are varied: a few attempt to overcome it through an act of will or intelligence; many ignore it, thinking it will go away; most hold on to a hope, a hope for a full recovery here or a better life beyond. These responses are by no means exhaustive of the number of human possibilities. Perhaps in a real way, human history, if Freud is correct in his *Civilization and Its Discontents*, is a series of systematized responses to what James has called "the worm at the core."

In America, for some time now, I think we have attempted to systematize our attitudes toward death. Not too many years ago H.L. Mencken said that if we were to go to the library and look under "Death: Human" in the card catalog, we'd be surprised at how few books there are on the subject. In those simpler times the way most of us chose to deal with death was by ignoring it.

By the mid-1960's, however, through a heightened sense of an endangered ecology, the ever-present possibility of nuclear annihilation, or perhaps through a sense that our increasingly permissive society was surely headed for disaster, numerous books, pamphlets, monographs, lectures, sensitivity groups, college courses, and self-help programs began to appear, all ostensibly designed to help us "deal" with death. It became fashionable for the new "thanatologists" to look back on Mencken's time as an era when "death was for Americans what sex was for the Victorians." Developmental stages of dying and slogans like "death with dignity" began to disperse our silence about mortality. The talking cure had hit the Grim Reaper.

Now in the throes of this enlightened age, we are admonished to "accept death with peace and equinimity" because it is "part of the life process." We seem to have moved from a denial of death in the 50's to a dance with death in the 70's. Unfortunately, the dance we are doing may be the tango, where, as you know, you take one step forward followed by two back. Rather than ignoring the dying, we now tell them what stage they are supposed to be in. We seem to have forgotten that people will invariably deal with death only as effectively and sensitively as they have dealt with other crisis situations their entire lives. I only wonder if Dylan Thomas didn't have a better handle on death than quite a few humanistic psychologists do these days. He advised us: "Do not go gentle into that good night/Rage, rage against the dying of the light."

Commentar, Winter 1980.

Free at Last

I had never noticed how much birch leaves look like human hands: fine, sap-filled veins coursing like the faint purple blood vessels which appear just below the layers of human baklava that is our skin.

The other morning as I lay on a grassy, sun-drenched knoll I looked up into a delicate, white birch that swayed with an exquisite grace in the early fall breeze. After a few moments, a solitary golden leaf silently detached itself and with an erratic wavering began its soundless journey to the earth. As a small child I believed the autumn leaves disconnected themselves only at night, preferring to save the special and poignant moment of release for their own kind.

But now, in a waning late September sun, I was slient witness as a scorched-yellow leaf found the freedom to which it had strained since late spring. It would no longer twist and strain at its tethering stem whenever stiff summer breezes blew.

In the moment it took the leaf to reach the ground, absolute liberty was its only possession -- but it was, mysteriously enough, at liberty to die. In early summer it had owned a different freedom, a living liberty where life juices flowed to the ends of radiating estuaries. By late September, it had achieved its new freedom, a freedom that was no longer tight-fastened and circumscribed: total liberty had come at the cost of its brevity. Still, something seemed right about the leaf's trading of one kind of freedom for another, more fleeting though just as real.

This morning I attended a memorial service held in honor of a dead colleague. He was a man I did not know well, but one I sensed I nevertheless understood. He had been poet, teacher, husband, administrator and part-time whirling dervish. He had been artist, father, friend and experimental film maker with far more ideas than the available celluloid could possibly hold.

For the last several months he had been a cancer patient. Week after painful week he had valiantly attempted to stave off his final twisting of the stem. He had tried chemotherapy, radiation and various other experimental treatments, all with little or no success. Without complaining, he had paid his share of the $250 billion a year spent in this country on cancer treatment.

Finally, a few weeks ago, he had had enough. Unlike most of the rest of us who, on average, will spend the last 40 days of our lives in hospitals, our souls twisting and turning on plastic stems hooked to vast machines, he decided to return home to his family.

In the hospital he had felt the ever present conflict between a terror of isolation and the desire to be left alone. At home he stayed quite comfortable: he gave advice to students, he loved family and friends, he talked of films he might have made. The morning he died he was wheeled outside and watched some early autumn leaves fall from the trees in his back yard. A little while later, something seemed right about trading one kind of liberty for another. And so he did.

Baltimore Evening Sun, October, 1984.

TRAVEL

A voyage to a destination, wherever it may be, is also a voyage inside oneself; even as a cyclone carries along with it the center in which it must ultimately come to rest.

-- Laurens Van Der Post

Love, Y.B.

I have just returned from what one of the major airlines calls a "getaway vacation." I got away to Cairo, while my bags got away to Athens.

The whole affair resembles the apocryphal story of the man who rushes to the airport ticket counter and breathlessly exclaims, "I want to go to Cairo, my wife to Athens and our luggage to Hong Kong."

"Well, I'm very sorry sir but we can't possibly arrange that," the ticket salesperson responded incredulously.

"Why not?" countered the traveler, "You did it last week."

Unfortunately, I am unmarried. Consequently, I have no wife to send to Athens. But if I did have a spouse, I might have managed to make the entire joke come true.

The worst part of this experience was not, as you might suspect, the fact that I was forced to inhabit the same pair of underwear for several days, nor that I was left to brush my teeth with my index finger and borrowed toothpaste. No, the real tragedy of the story lies in the fact that my bags seem to have had a better time than I did. But already I am getting ahead of myself in this tale.

We, me and my bags, parted company at National Airport on a Sunday. It was not a tearful goodbye. I did not hold on to the handles of my luggage longer than I should have as it disappeared from sight down the little conveyor belt and through the hole in the wall with the flapping pieces of clear plastic behind the check-in counter. I was under the mistaken impression we would only be apart for a few hours -- that we were merely sitting in different compartments of the same plane.

By Monday, I was ogling the majestic pyramids. My bags were nowhere to be found. Cairo is a city of 12 million people. There is housing for only about eight million of them. The other four million hang around at the airport.

Most of them bring a friend. This makes it very difficult to find anything in the Cairo airport, except a crowd.

The woman at the lost luggage counter was tall and dark. She wore a red and blue company tie that had been contorted into a bizarre parody of a Windsor knot when she examined my claim stubs and solved the mystery of my bags' whereabouts. The stubs were for two pieces of luggage sent to Athens. She said the people in Washington do this all the time.

I began to hiss and screw my mouth up into a hideous pout -- the way I would when this sort of thing happens in the states. Back home this is usually a prelude to my screaming about inefficiency and asking to see someone's supervisor. But then a uniformed man carrying a Russian-made machine gun and patch on his arm which said "Tourist Police" in Arabic stepped in and asked the lady if he should shoot me. In Arabic she said, "No," or possibly, "Not just yet." She then assured me I would have my bags back by Tuesday, since there was a flight coming from Athens to Cairo that afternoon.

On Tuesday there was no word from the airlines. I decided to turn my underwear inside out and stoically to hope for the best. I also visited a number of breathtaking Egyptian monuments which allowed me to forget about my misfortune for a while. I did, however, find myself sitting alone on the back of the bus, two seats separating me from the nearest tourists. They had apparently decided the shirt I had worn for four days in the Cairo heat was also breathtaking. One only has so much breath to be taken before the results are very serious.

In the mail on Wednesday, I received a picture postcard from the Acropolis. On the reverse side, in very steady black ink, was penned, "Having a terrific time. Some extraordinary vistas. Wish you were here. Love, Your Bags."

Thursday I began a cruise up the Nile. I was stopped on the gangplank by the captain who politely asked me if I would mind terribly leaving my underwear back in Cairo. It stood on the dock all by itself when we departed. It did not wave.

By Saturday, we had steamed into Aswan. There another postcard awaited my arrival. On the front was a picture of the Parthenon. On the back the text read: "Having a fantastic time. This is so exhilirating. Wish you were here. Y.B."

On Monday, back at the hotel, there was another postcard waiting for me. It was a picture of two people wind surfing on the Mediterranean sea. On the back was another message:

"The food is exquisite. The weather could not be more idyllic. ("Idyllic" was scratched out and misspelled several times.) Y.B."

The ignominity of this whole affair was starting to get to me. The notion of taking separate vacations had been stretched beyond its breaking point. I sulked in the elevator on the way up to my room where, to my amazement, I found both of my bags lounging on the bed. They were suntanned and had stickers on which were printed messages like "I climbed Mt. Olympus," all over them.

I must admit, they both looked very good, though they did have a rather worn look, an exhaustion undisplayed the last time I had seen them. I opened both bags to make sure everything was there. It was all as I had left it, except the thesaurus, which seemed much older and mysteriously well-worn.

Baltimore Evening Sun, June, 1984.

Where the Heavens Meet the Sea

On this Scottish coast, from late fall to winter's end, the sea trades shades of grey with the sky it meets on the indefinable horizon. It is not colors they exchange. It is a catalog of almost indescribable variations somewhere between steel grey and spent charcoal. One day the ocean seems darker, more malevolent than the overcast firmament. The next morning the sky is more ominous -- full of clenched fists ready to strike incautious fishermen. Only clouds have this particular way of frightening. They loom up like spectres, telling a tale of more foul weather to come, or perhaps just reminding one of a storm that has long been brewing in the soul. In this atmosphere, where the vast penetrating greyness is stretched out for all those who will look, it is sometimes possible, indeed advisable, to let one's fears remain uncovered.

In these months, the sun is a rare and welcome intruder in this troubled grey region, where one is inevitably reminded of the ambiguous seascapes and portentious grey fowl of Melville's *Benito Cereno*. There is no whiteness of the whale here, all is grey, shifting from darker to light and back again. On those rare occasions in mid-day when the sun becomes visible, the sea and sky respond by exchanging translucent shades of aquamarine and pastel blue. On these special mornings, the ocean flattens out, electricity seems to course and skip lightly on its shimmering surface. Tiny irridescent whitecaps send faint ripples gliding to the shore.

But the winter mornings when the sun makes its courageous appearance can be counted on the digits of my woolen mittens. Most days are like this one: bleak, silent, solitary. Hours are spent staring from inside the house at the vast grey sea. One places bets on which raindrops will win the race to the bottom of the window pane. It is another of nature's ironies -- the winners cease to exist, while the more stable drops never move, eventually freezing, victims of their own inactivity.

Looking out the window, low tide unfolds. A thousand tiny, moss-green islands appear adjacent to the narrow stone pier that juts out stoically into the sea for a few hundred yards. The grey and earthen colored pier of rock and cement ends abruptly at a sea wall. Those who have created it, and those who have continually sustained it over the last eight centuries, know you can only go so far. There is never any confusion among the pier workers and the great sea about who is the master and who are the servants.

In high tide these small continents will disappear like a thousand miniature Atlantises. The seagulls will again anticipate the shifting of the tide, and move from their mossy perches closer to the shore in search of food. These birds never divulge the secret of the *terra incognita.* For these few hours, the tiny islands will remain as hidden as any lost land.

But in the evening of some exceptional winter days, sometimes just before sundown, one can discover an invisible thread that ties the earth to the sky. On these special days, though sunrise to day's end may have been lost in the terrible greyness, at dusk the horizon clears, revealing a collection of scarlet and magenta hues not fashioned in this world. The sun offers both sea and sky a gift of translucent beauty. And it is in these few moments before the darkness descends that one can almost believe that off in the great distance one might eventually arrive at a divine point, where the heavens really do meet the sea.

🍇 Unpublished, January 1984.

X,Y,Zed

Winston Churchill or George Bernard Shaw or some other famous English person once remarked that Great Britain and the United States are two lands permanently separated by the use of a common language. This comment was occasioned, I think, not just by the obvious fact that some say "po-tay-toe," while others prefer "po-taa-toe." The remark points to a much more profound and fundamental cleavage in our shared tongue.

I don't begrudge the British their rather idiosyncratic names for french fries (chips), flashlights (torches) and ovens (cookers). I can even go along with calling trashmen "binmen," erasers "rubbers" and their insistence that "washing up" refers to dishes, while "cleaning up" is done in connection with personal hygiene. The linguistic line must be drawn, however, at calling cookies "biscuits." Imagine a Biscuit Monster on Sesame Street. Bert and Ernie would laugh him right off the stage.

In Great Britain a "flat" is an apartment. I discovered recently you should never offer to fix someone's flat in London. "Braces" are suspenders and "suspenders" are garter belts. Since this is a family newspaper I can't begin to describe the difficulties this confusion has caused me.

"Lifts" are elevators which means it becomes practically impossible to offer someone a lift, unless of course you are quite philanthropic or perhaps mechanically inclined. It is true that it is very easy to figure out who wears the pants in the British family. "Pants" are underwear.

After a few months of careful observation, I am now prepared to make some tentative conclusions about the possible roots of this linguistic perplexion among the English, Scots and Welsh. They at once begin to be understood when one comes to realize that the people of the United Kingdom use a different alphabet than we do in the United States.

It is true that the first 25 letters are precisely the same in both places. But the people of Great Britain call the 26th and last letter, a "zed." Of course, all one has to do is sing the alphabet song out loud to discern who has the proper pronunciation of this final consonant. "Q,R,S and T,U,V; W, and X,Y,Zed?" Can you imagine Zorro robbing from the rich and giving to the poor, while always leaving his trademark, the sign of the zed? Obviously, it loses something vital in the translation.

The fact that the last letter of the British alphabet has such a creepy sound to it has led the people of the United Kingdom to go to extraordinary lengths to avoid having to use the zed. Consequently, a perfectly good word like "realize" has been turned into the rather innocuous looking "realise." Similar surgery has been performed to produce "legalise", "categorise", and "civilisation." All to save the British the embarrassment of having to say "Zed" if some unknowing individual were to ask them to spell one or more of these words.

I am still in the process of discovering what all this has to do with the fact that trucks are called "lorries" in the United Kingdom. Consequently, the big, burly, tattooed gentlemen who steer these huge vehicles through the streets and "dual carriageways" of Britian are called "lorry drivers."

Can you imagine these guys pulling their 18-wheel rigs into a "lorry stop?" Neither can I. In fact, the men of this profession long ago found the name lorry so embarrassing that they vowed to always drive their trucks on the left side of the road. Needless to say, this immediately converted all the other fearful motorists of Great Britain to that side as well, which, of course, brings us to the origin of another strange, nonlinguistic, British practice of driving on the wrong side of the road.

Baltimore Evening Sun, August, 1984.

Cairo: Land of Kismet

Cairo. The first and most lasting impression is surely the dust. It is everywhere. It blows in on the *khamsin,* a burning wind that comes from the south, or, in the spring, is supplied by the more violent *sobaa,* a north African kin of the *sirocco,* which sometimes closes down the airport and turns everything the color of sand. The golden dust is ubiquitous, as ever-present as the modern Egyptian's laid back and well measured interpretation of *kismet,* the will of *Allah.* Fine yellow sand is caked on the windows of the French metros, Italian trolleys and the Egyptian-made buses that go into the making of an endless traffic free-for-all that is Cairo. Here the automobile horn has superceded the brake system as the most indispensable part of the Cairene's car. This is a city of 12 million people, yet a place where no lane lines can be found painted on city streets or even the largest of highways. Traffic lights are only more or less obeyed; the one unbendable rule of the roads is "watch your front."

But despite the frenzy of most of Cairo's drivers, it is a city that permanently moves at 33 1/3. It is a place where an estimated one to two million people live in the larger crypts of its two major cemeteries. The living do little to disturb the dead. The dead seem to return the favor. Here the difference between living and dying is only a matter of degree.

The word for "fast" seems little used in Egyptian Arabic, save for its sensible and benign utilization during the holy month of *Ramadan.* Sleeping dogs and drowsy old men in full-length, cotton *galabayas* compete for the shade of city street corners. They sleep away the afternoon heat that sometimes reaches 110 degrees. It is the kind of heat that instantly turns all foreigners into thermal statisticians or melting souls who attempt to magically ward off its searing effect by announcing to anyone who will listen that it is a "dry" heat.

The scrawny dogs and somnolent men are never molested, except by the dizzy and lethargic flies whose laconic wings even seem to beat less quickly here. In the late afternoon, all that exists is the intense heat, the everlasting traffic jam, and groups of black-clad women who patiently sit in clusters waiting for buses that run on a time-table known only to the prophet Mohammed and perhaps a few of his closer associates. These women sit apart from their husbands, huddled together in black cotton garments that conceal all but their faces. Their attire and position give them the impression of having been dumped at the bus stops in ebony sacks.

Cairo. It is a city that for over 5,000 years has watched over the great pyramids of Giza. These massive triangular structures, constituted of large parts of pharaonic necrophilia and billions of grains of the same compressed golden sand, seem majestically to ignore the pungent smell of camel dung, and the litanies of hawkers selling soft drinks, photographic slides, and a well practiced bedouin image infused with a little too much of the Fuller brush salesman for most Western tastes.

The pyramids, and many of the other equally impressive ancient monuments to the intelligence and sophistication of the early Egyptians, give mute but eloquent testimony to the ironic truth of just how far Egyptian civilization seems to have fallen in 5,000 years of history.

Today cholera scares are as frequent as the pipe leaks that regularly flood the streets with raw sewage and corrode the antiquated power and telephone cables beneath the city. The state-owned television company offers two stations, 12 hours a day. One channel is educational, the other serves up Arabic soap operas and 1950's Egyptian-made movies with endless chase scenes through the streets of a far less congested Cairo, as well as panoramic visions of the Nile, and corpulent, Western-clad gentlemen replete with pencil thin moustaches and fezes.

An international phone call is usually a futile exercise, often resembling something from the middle of a John Cage concert. The correct number for the largest hotel in Cairo remains a mystery even to the Egyptian operators. Many Cairenes attempt to solve some of the communication problems inherent in a city that lacks a published telephone directory by posting their numbers on the walls of their homes. This may be the only city in the world where everyone has an unpublished number.

The population of modern Egypt has increased 1,000 percent in the last century, while the inhabitable land has not yet doubled since the time of the Greeks. The government points with pride to its annual gross national product growth rate of 8 percent, but that seems small when measured against the addition of a million people a year in the city of Cairo alone.

If these people do share anything at all with their ancient countrymen it is the mystery that there is, clinging to these narrow banks of the Nile, a people at all -- a people who go on despite what seem like colossal impediments to life. In ancient times these obstacles came in the form of foreign invaders and nature itself. Today these same impediments are still present, but they have been joined by an unchecked growth in this culture that lives with one foot each implanted deeply in two very different ways of life. The one is old, full of character, and clearly Egyptian. The other is new, Western, and sometimes ill-fitting.

The most spoken word in the tourist haunts of Cairo is "welcome". It is spoken by taxi drivers, shop owners and children on the streets. But welcome has brought with it *baksheesh,* a once noble but now corrupted Arabic word that has come to be synonymous with "tip." With the arrival of *baksheesh,* one gets the impression that these people have become Egyptians pretending to be what Western tourists think Egyptians should be.

The result is the strangest kind of nature imitating art. The people who by choice or necessity have begun to make their livings through contact with foreigners seem oddly out of focus, like the lime-green and pale yellow faces that stare from the billboards lining many of Cairo's streets. These hawkers seek *baksheesh* not so much in exchange for the collection of camel dolls, tennis hats and cheap figurines they sell, as for the well-orchestrated performance they give as Egyptians.

It is this kind of split -- between the few short and veiled glimpses one is allowed to get of the complex and richly variegated people the Egyptians most surely are, and the one-dimensional, comic masks worn by them for the edification of tourists -- that perhaps is most disturbing. One wishes to see these pyramids, and the people who have lived for 50 centuries in their shadows, after the sightseers have all gone away. One longs for a look at what these noble people must have been like before time was measured in the intervals between the arrival of tour buses.

Baltimore Evening Sun, August, 1984.

Ambience

Do you remember when the only connotations the letters 'a' and 'm' had in the English language were as the first person singular present tense form of the verb to be, and as an aid in keeping time? For years this sturdy pair had worked side by side as an ontological team, ushering in and out of existence the veritable furniture and wall paper of the universe; and when separated and completed by two skimpy periods, hardly any help at all, this versatile vowel and hardworking consonant had unerringly indicated when it was not yet noon.

Well, no longer will we think of these servicable letters only in connection with Popeye's tautological response to Olive Oyl or with the rather mysterious reply God gave to Moses' query in Exodus regarding what the Divine name might be, and occasionally with certain colleges and universities devoted to animal husbandry. Now it seems 'a' and 'm' are also working overtime as a prefix for any noun even remotely associated with the company formerly known as the Pennsylvania Railroad.

Amtrak, in an effort to get America into training, has added a patriotic mantra to all things railroad. It is now possible to secure an amsaver which entitles you to a seat on one of the amcoaches which comprise the amfleet which also includes an amclub car to which you might amble in search of an amsnack which, unfortunately, tastes like something manufactured by Amway.

And this amnosis doesn't stop with the purchase of your ticket. Once seated on the train, people have begun involuntarily to speak Amlatin. On a recent trip to New York two very normal native English speakers, an elderly couple from Washington, could be heard describing the shrubbery whizzing by as "ambushes."

Two Freudian psychoanalysts on their way to a conference in Philadelphia hotly debated some of the finer points of the structure of human consciousness, complete with amid and amego. By the time the amsteward inquired as to whether I would like some amice to freshen up my amcocktail, I had had enough.

Somewhere outside of Newark I began to wonder if we should so uncritically accept the use of this new *lingua traina*. In this time of rising unemployment do we really want two frail, little letters working three jobs? It hardly seems fair.

We almost never employ 'q' and 'x'. Let them work for the railroad. Think of all the possibilities for a logo. The 'x' even looks like a little railroad crossing. If we hired 'q' and 'x' for the railroad job we'd be getting them both off the welfare roles and out of the unemployment line. "Qxtrak." It has a kind of ring to it. It calls to mind those speedy French and Japanese trains. I think we may really have something here; all those in favor of "Qxtrak" say amamen.

🌿 *Baltimore Evening Sun,* March, 1983.

The Pyramids -- From a Couch

When I was a small child there was a particular sort of ache that would come on in my knees whenever I had been in church for any longer than 30 minutes.

In those days the mass was longer, a kind of nonecumenical endurance test. Consequently, one could quite easily discern succeeding generations of devout Catholics by how they didn't kneel in church. The very young knelt bolt upright, looking more or less like small, human embodiments of the capital letter L. The middleaged, after many years of Tridentine consecrations and benedictions, had by now collapsed into a kind of ecclesistical compromise - butts rested lightly on the backs of pews but knees still firmly in place, a tired but devout transition to the approximation of large and small case C's. The elderly, perhaps more pragmatic and resigned after years of groaning ligaments, knew somehow the Almighty would not mind their sitting through the entire service.

In church I came to expect pain in my patellas. But now, years later, that same feeling comes on in my knees when I am forced to inhabit a department store for longer than ten minutes. What is perhaps worse is that I have discovered recently it also returns when I am sight-seeing.

This admission is not an easy one to make. When sightseeing my intentions are always initially quite noble. A man may be measured by the places he has been. Unfortunately, when I spend more than 30 minutes in any of a variety of cultural haunts and places of historical interest, my knees begin to send me a painful message. I gather I am not alone in this affliction. In fact, if you look carefully into the eyes of supposedly eager tourists you are more likely to find, I suspect, what Henry James recognized many years ago while watching a gaggle of Americans shuffling around the National Gallery: "Their faces bear expressions of resentment, humanized by fatigue."

What really bothers me about sight-seeing, however, is how the actual sites -- the pyramids, a cathedral, the ruins of a medieval castle -- silently and effortlessly go on making their enormous statements with no real exertion on their part, while by a sheer act of the will the spectators are left to do all the work. The fact that a long time ago an awful lot of work went into the making of the Taj Mahal or Westminster Abbey does nothing to dilute the disparity.

I suppose the real issue that needs to be dealt with is why I feel so guilty when my knees begin to groan. My high brow cranium just can't convince my philistine patellas they really are having a wonderful time.

All of this had led me to the rather somber conclusion there is still much work to be done in the area of psychiatric orthopedics. Neurotic patella fatigue is a disease we still know so little about. We do know that it only affects culturally enlightened people who are supposed to be having a good time. Perhaps one stop-gap measure would be to place a series of couches alongside St. Peter's, the Great Wall of China, etc., each staffed with an understanding orthopedic psychiatrist or paraprofessional especially trained for the treatment of NPF.

Of course, this is just an emergency measure. We can't expect these health care professionals to get to the root of the problem in one 50-minute hour. But it will get these patients off their feet, and temporarily alleviate some of the strain between them and their patellas.

Baltimore Evening Sun, July, 1984.

*B*roken Things

> I thought that nature was enough
> Till human nature came.
> -- Emily Dickinson

There is a spot on the eastern coast of Scotland, between the ancient fishing villages of Anstruther and Crail, where things mercilessly disappear. It is a place that displays a simple but clear maxim: nature has no heart. She, like many other beauties, is so often credited with kindness because of her countenance, but rarely for the deeds she performs in this place.

One arrives at this spot, as I did last year at this time, by traversing an extremely narrow, switch-back path which eventually descends to a dark, uncaring and incomprehensibly powerful North Sea. On rare clear days, at this coastal place, huge, jagged, algae-covered rocks can be detected lying treacherously just below the surface of the water. Anything reaching the narrow beach which hugs the base of a broad, earthen colored crag must first be dragged across these dangerous submerged stones. Those shells and pieces of driftwood not destroyed in the maelstrom of sharp rock and churning sea eventually find their unceremonious and silent end in an abrupt and violent impact with sheer-faced, moss-covered boulders that line the beach. For most living things traveling to this spot, this is the end of the line.

When I hike to this shore, no matter what the weather, shivers are sent coursing through my body. This is a dangerous and unfeeling place. It is one of those spots where the living, the dead, and the living-dead are all treated with the same kind of egalitarian, but ferocious, constancy.

On that sand, even on the quietest of mornings, no shell is found unbroken. Splintered wood is found strewn everywhere. Nothing remains whole. The bones of gulls and incautious Scottish fisherman have been pounded for centuries into that ochre colored beach.

Since my return to the states, it is not often I think of Scotland. Classes, faculty meetings, student papers which seem to asexually reproduce themselves atop my desk, and the exigencies of what is sometimes called the "real world" all conspire to keep me from these thoughts.

The other morning, however, I was reminded of that spot on the Scottish coast, the place where things disappear. I was traveling north on Calvert Street, part of a rolling ocean of humanity on its way to work, when I spotted some of the broken things: grey-overcoated men wrapped in plastic and huddled together like the charcoal colored, broken-winged ducks I had spotted washed up on the bleak Scottish coast.

These men, their deeply lined faces matching the ashen color of their soiled coats, can be found in early morning clinging to the heating vents of municipal buildings or sprawled atop manhole covers, billows of wispy white smoke seeming to emanate from their swollen limbs. Before the business day, at that time and place, few things can be found left unbroken.

As the traffic light changed, I instinctively reached to turn up the heater. Then, I began to move again with the flow of cars -- a silent drop encased in steel and glass traveling in an incomprehensible and uncaring ocean. Through the rear view mirror I spied a bent-up man with a shopping cart full of cast off objects -- broken things discarded by less broken lives. On the opposite corner, I looked back at the huddled men. I know they have many stories to tell about broken things and about those places where things disappear.

Baltimore Evening Sun, November, 1984.

Minding My Queues

It has always been a source of no little confusion to me that people in New York stand on line, while the rest of the inhabitants of North America stand in line. Because for years I have secretly harbored this conumdrum in my soul, I am now quite susceptible to musings about the way people around the globe gather and are served in public places: in Germany, the swiftest are always served first in banks, post office, etc.; in Italy, one is inevitably bumped forward until reaching the teller; in Great Britain, people do not stand in line, nor will you find them on line, unless you have chanced upon a computer enthusiast deep in the throes of his addiction. In the British Isles, they queue up -- for everything. The word "queue" is itself a kind of self referential metaphor for the way people can be found *en masse* in England, Scotland and Wales. If you will notice, the letters 'q', 'u' and 'e' would actually be quite sufficient to spell queue. In fact, just the single letter 'q' would do the trick. But somehow or other, because it is Great Britain, a series of 'u's' and 'e's' have begun to line up behind the solitary 'q'. It is a kind of queue behind the 'q', as it were. Indeed, if you are reading this anywhere in the United Kingdom, by the time it takes you to reach the bottom of the page, there will be, more than likely, an entire rigid gaggle of 'u's' and 'e's' standing redundantly but obediently to the rear of that initial 'q'.

Indeed, this obdurate precision is perhaps the most amazing aspect of the British penchant for the queue. Unlike other nations, the British always stand directly behind each other, unerringly allowing 18 inches between themselves and the person in front. One gets 18 inches -- whether you have queued up to meet the Queen or to purchase some pickled herring.

In the United Kingdom, there is no notion of a conceptual queue, no loose idea of who was ahead of whom. In England, people can always be found precisely situated, one behind the other, shoulders square up. This often makes for some bizarre sights. Many bus stops throughout Britain, for example, are equipped with an overhang that allows people waiting for transport to stay dry in inclement weather. These waiting areas, under normal conditions, should accommodate 10 to 15 people. Inevitably, on rainy days, however, one can discover four or five people, one behind the other, dry and comfy under the protection of the overhang, while to the rear of the queue can be found 10 to 12 drenched but stoic souls.

An even stranger scene is the sight of half a dozen sleepy but orderly ghosts queued up in the middle of the night in an otherwise deserted British railway station. The rest of the country sleeps and these six people stand one behind the other, looking like lost French Foreign Legionnaires lined up for a parade in the middle of the night.

Until quite recently, I thought that much of this business about the inflexibility of the British queue was my own rather vivid imagination. But then the other day, while standing in line for confession, I changed my mind. As I inched toward the box, making sure to leave the required 18 inches between me and the penitent in front, I heard a small voice from inside the confessional plaintively whisper, "Bless me Father for I have sinned, I failed to queue up at the Post Office." The priest, in a sympathetic tone, began to respond: "You will recall, my child, the words of the Lord, 'Whenever two or more are gathered in My name, they must queue up.'" With that, I began to feel dizzy, as if I had been given a glimpse of the choirs of angels and saints, but all lined up and in alphabetical order. Immediately, I ran to the back of the church to make a frantic escape, but I was stopped short by a brusk and officious looking elderly woman. I had barged into the queue for the holy water fount.

🍂 Unpublished, October, 1983.

*L*ife and Death in Scotland

Some landscapes seem stubbornly to refuse history. Some efface it so completely, it is never to be found again. In still others, there is a partial subjugation, where nature seems to leave just enough of the past that it effectively subdues the living, or at the very least holds them in a temporary spell.

This morning, at dawn, I walked to the edge of the North Sea. As my toes sank into the sand and pebbles of the St. Andrews shore, a huge, perfectly round ball of orange light had slowly begun to make its way from beneath the sea of rippled glass stretched out before me.

Above and to the left of where I stood there looms a great cliff, full of half-embedded boulders that hang precariously to the face of this huge earthen-colored crag. The cliff is only partially hidden by strategically placed snow fences and carefully lettered red and white signs warning of erosion and falling rock.

To the right stand the ruins of a great medieval cathedral. All but its walls have been destroyed, now nearly 500 years. Another few hundred yards up the coast can be found the sparse remains of an ancient castle whose earliest masonry work dates from the beginning of the 13th century.

It was on this site in 1546 that Cardinal David Beaton, after a leisurely lunch, sat calmly digesting his food while he watched George Wishart being burned at the stake for the crime of heresy. A few months later, while the Cardinal was not so calmly fortifying the castle against the expected onslaughts of the reformers, several Protestants, posing as stone masons, murdered the cleric in his chambers and hung the body by a single arm and leg from the wall head.

A hundred years later, all but the castle walls and a lone tower had suffered the same fate as the Cardinal. A little more still survives of it gutted neighbor to the south, the cathedral.

At sunrise, the present seems not to exist on this Scottish coast. The newly created shadows from the ruins appear and one is reminded of the slow but inevitable reclamation that is going on: nature is methodically and unceremoniously effacing this small part of history.

As I allow myself to become privy to that process, I am reminded at once that human beings are not all that natural. All that I share with the seagulls who glide to furtive and tangential stops on our shared beach is the brevity of our stays. On that shore, at that hour, the inevitable future becomes married to the distant past. They both seem a good deal more real than the present.

I am startled out of my reverie by a solitary fisherman. His steel grey eyes seem to appreciate my surprise and embarrassment. I stare up at the cathedral and inquire, "Do you suppose it lasted as long as they thought it would?" "It never does," he answered. And I walked back to the road alone.

Baltimore Evening Sun, November, 1983.

SCIENCE

If physical science is dangerous as I have said, it is dangerous because it necessarily ignores the idea of moral evil.

-- *John Henry Newman*

Theology as Biology

In mid-May, during one of his nationally televised sermons, the Reverend Jerry Falwell boasted that a recent action by the Virginia State Board of Education would enable graduates of his Liberty Baptist College to teach biblical creationism in the Virginia public school classrooms.

Although the school board saw its meeting April 8 as an effort to answer the question of the certification of Liberty Baptist's biology graduates as teachers in the Virginia public school system, Mr. Falwell saw in the deliberations a larger design: "So now we, with God's help, want to see hundreds of our graduates go out into the classroom and teach creationism."

It is, of course, unlikely that Virginia school children will be flipping through Genesis 1-3 in Biology 101. Chan Kendrick, the director of the Virginia Chapter of the American Civil Liberties Union, moved quickly in the wake of Mr. Falwell's reaction to the school board action and pressured the board to postpone any further action on the Liberty Baptist students.

The latest effort by Mr. Falwell, when viewed in isolation, seems insignificant, but when seen in the light of the recent federal District Court's decision to overturn the Arkansas law requiring the teaching of creationism, it indicates the kind of tenacity shown by those who would have creationism -- the Bible -- taught in the public schools.

Why is there such doggedness of purpose among the creationists? What lies at the heart of this quest to establish creationism in the public school system? In examining comments made by Henry Morris, the director of the Institute for Creation Research, as well as remarks made by Kelley and Nell Seagraves, the cofounders of the Creation Science Research Center, there appear to be at least three major fears at the center of the creationist's zeal.

First, the creationists seem to be particularly concerned with the ramifications evolutionary theory may have for one of the traditional arguments for the existence of God, the teleological proof. In brief, this argument suggests that it can be demonstrated that God exists because the universe shows the handiwork of a grand designer. "Everything fits together marvelously in a grand scheme," William Paley asserted in his 18th century classic, *Natural Theology*. Consequently, adaptions occur rarely and only by Divine fiat.

The design argument became particularly vulnerable, the creationists believe, after the advent of evolutionary theory, because adaptions began to be understood in terms of natural selection. Usefulness and design began to be understood by the new biologists as effect, rather than cause.

Ironically, the creationists have never been very good students of history. David Hume and Immanuel Kant, two 18th century philosophers, had levelled telling criticisms of Paley's teleological argument almost 100 years before the writing of Charles Darwin's *The Origins of Species* in 1859.

More importantly, the creationists seem never to have examined another way out of this design dilemma. Asa Gray, a Harvard botanist, had suggested that we might broaden the concept of design by applying it to the evolutionary process as a whole, rather than specific organisms or species. He intelligently defended a compromise position between evolution and fundamentalism, producing a theory of God's gradually unfolding design. His suggestion avoids both the specific criticisms of Kant and Hume, and still allows for the creationist concern that God is acting in history.

A second fear associated with the creationist zeal may be seen in the following remark by Nell Seagraves: "The naturalist-humanist-atheists are running this country...If you teach that man is an animal the way evolutionists do, then there is no right and no wrong and people will act like animals."

It should be clear that Mrs. Seagraves, as well as other committed creationists, sees Darwinism as undermining our fundamental human dignity and uniqueness.

It is true that Darwin and his immediate followers tended to minimize the differences between human beings and other animals. Darwin saw most of man's distinctive capabilities as products of natural selection. It is of some interest, however, that A.R. Wallace, who had formulated the principle of natural selection independently but concomitantly with Darwin, recognized in his later writings that his theory could not account for what he called "man's higher faculties." Dr. Wallace suggested "...natural selection could only have endowed savage man with a brain a little superior to the ape, whereas he actually possesses one very little inferior to the philosopher."

Wallace also was troubled by man's musical, artistic and ethical capabilities that often contribute nothing to survival. He suggested "Some Higher Intelligence may have directed the process by which the human race was developed." Although many successive biologists and philosophers have disagreed with Wallace's supposition, it is important to recognize that the only two alternatives in this debate are not creationist theism or "naturalist-humanist-atheist."

The third, and perhaps most important, fear of the creationists is that Darwin's theory directly challenges the notion of biblical inerrancy. Ironically, long before the mid-19th century, biblical literalism had been cast in doubt. The dismantling of the ptolemaic universe by Copernicus in the 16th century saw the beginning of its demise.

In the 18th century, the development of the new science of geology cast further doubts on the viability of biblical inerrancy as a logically consistent point of view. A concurrent development, the rise of modern biblical scholarship, of which Voltaire and John Locke were notable early members, proved to be the end of this rigid form of biblical inspiration.

Reaching its culmination in the work of Julius Wellhausen, a late 19th century biblical scholar, the historical and literary method known as "higher criticism" began to show to those people willing to look that the text contains a number of anachronisms, repeated narratives, contradictions and marked changes in style and syntax. All these discoveries led most reputable scholars of the late 19th century, and now as well, to the opinion that the Old Testament is a rich, multi-layered collection of documents.

But the creationists see themselves backed in a corner. The only way to defend their point of view is to resort to a thinly veiled doctrine of biblical inerrancy.

Curiously enough, the evolutionists of the late 19th century may have had a hand in framing this particular fear expressed by creationists. Many of the leading scientists of Darwin's day began to link evolution explicitly to their own agnostic or atheistic theological positions. Conservative Christians found themselves seemingly left with no other alternative but to oppose evolutionary theory. For the biblical literalist, there could be no reasonable compromise. Genesis described the one-time creation of all species in their present form.

This rigidity, openly encouraged by biologists in the generation following Darwin, eventually led thinkers like Phillip Gosse to propose that God had put various strata of fossils in a misleading evolutionary pattern to test the faith of Christians.

Although evolutionary thinkers of the 19th century may have invited the battle lines on biblical inspiration to be drawn so starkly, there were other thinkers of the last century whose views of scripture allowed for the acceptance of divine participation in the text without accepting every jot and tittle as true.

The majority of Protestant theologians of the late 19th century began to distinguish between the religious or mythic insights of the text, and the ancient cosmologies through which these insights were expressed.

These men and women interpreted the biblical account as a symbolic and poetic affirmation of the absolute dependence of all of nature on God. Unlike the creationists, it is a point of view many critical and discerning Christians and Jews still find completely compatible with the picture so painstakenly given us by Charles Darwin.

> *Baltimore Sunday Sun,* August, 1982.

The Karen Quinlan Case

In America in the last decade or so it has become increasingly apparent that media function in at least two ways. First, newspapers and the electronic media report; they dispense information to a wide audience. The second function the media provide is commentary; they often present views of the news that conflict with the views of the newsmaker. This second function began to be evident in the early years of the conflict in Vietnam. It has been with us ever since.

The first function requires a kind of instantaneousness -- the initial report of a news story is usually considered the most important. But the effort to be first makes the media run the danger of not reporting reality, but rather shaping it.

In the recent Karen Quinlan case in New Jersey, the media both reported and commented. But in the rush to put a frame around the issues involved in the case, most if not all of the early reporters presented the wrong picture: they said the case involved the definition of death.

Karen Quinlan, 20, has been on a respirator for some months. Her parents have gone through a lengthy legal process to obtain permission from the courts to disconnect the respirator, which would allow her to die. On March 31, the New Jersey Supreme Court ruled the parents could disconnect the respirator if physicians agreed the respirator should be removed.

Early television newscasts, however, as well as the press, repeatedly cast the Quinlan case in terms of new definitions of death, versus older, established definitions. But the Quinlan case was not then, nor is it now, involved with defining death. By no existing or proposed definition is Karen Quinlan dead.

However, the prosecutor of Morris County, N.J., Donald G. Collester Jr., said in an early interview, "This case raised the issue of the legal definition of death." A short time later, Governor Brendon Byrne of New Jersey was asked whether he favored a new statutory definition of death for his state. *The New York Times* printed his reply in a front page story, which appeared next to a lengthy report on the Quinlan case.

Newsweek, in an otherwise satisfactory account, included in its cover story on the Quinlan incident, "There is the question of when death occurs, and what standards should be used to define it."

Many journalists and newscasters have argued from the beginning of this case that if New Jersey had had a statutory definition similar to other states, Karen Quinlan's situation would have been resolved. This simply is not the case.

The other states in question (Maryland, Kansas, Michigan, Oregon, California, Virginia, Georgia, and New Mexico) have all patterned their definitions on criteria developed by an *ad hoc* committee at the Harvard Medical School, on the definition of brain death.

In 1968, this committee, chaired by Dr. Henry K. Beecher, formulated guidelines under which a physician may pronounce a patient dead if the patient shows an absence of brain waves on an electroencephalogram for 24 hours, together with a lack of spontaneous breathing, fixed and dilated pupils, and no response to external stimuli.

Karen Quinlan clearly does not fit the definition of death; and since that is the case, we must, of course, ask ourselves what is at issue here. The answer to this question would seem to lie in three distinct but related areas.

First, there is the area of the changing legal climate in terms of the practice of medicine and the ever increasing concern for the protection of the patient in American jurisprudence. Malpractice suits are rising at an astronomical level in the United States.

In 1975, Dr. Kenneth Edelin, a Boston ostretrician, was convicted of manslaughter for performing an abortion and not trying to save the life of the aborted fetus. Since then many physicians have become increasingly leery about their potential ability to cease treatment in a range of cases. This burden is thought by many physicians to be a handicap that not only seriously undermines the trust of the patient, but also limits the physician in terms of his or her primary responsibility, the welfare of the patient.

This issue is directly related to the Quinlan situation. Karen Quinlan's parents signed a release to permit physicians to turn off the respirator, but because of the fear of possible litigation, the physicians refused.

The second area involved in the Quinlan case is directly related to the first. Because the physicians feared possible litigation, they moved the situation from what essentially was a moral question to a legal one. This move itself raises the question of whether moral issues such as the Quinlan case should be resolved in the courts.

One way in which this question might be resolved is by looking at the third issue which seems to be at stake here. This third point is this: with new technological advancements, we have been successful in keeping alive people who in the past would most certainly have died.

In some areas of medicine, such as vaccination for disease, open heart surgery and transplants, this advancement has been just that -- a real moving ahead. In other cases, however, we have created machinery and procedures which have kept people alive with absolutely no hope for recovery.

Confounding this issue are the cases where it is crucial for the patient to have a say, but where the patient is incapable of speaking for himself. In our society, when someone cannot make decisions, that responsibility usually passes to the next of kin.

In Karen Quinlan's case, however, because of the threat of litigation, the physicians refused to act on the parent's request. Consequently, the decision making responsibility passed from the parents to a court-appointed guardian. With the April New Jersey Supreme Court decision, however, the decision making responsibility was returned to the parents.

The question of who makes the decision is a moral problem, not a legal one. The inability of American jurisprudence to make moral decisions on death and dying has a long history. For instance, in two Jehovah's Witnesses test cases concerning women with cancer, contradictory decisions were reached, although the cases were identical. In the first case, the courts decided a woman must seek treatment contrary to her religious convictions. In the other case, however, the courts reached the opposite conclusion: the woman was allowed not to seek treatment.

In the end, the New Jersey Supreme Court had the sense to realize that Karen Quinlan's parents were making a moral decision, one that perhaps should be unfettered by the sometimes lengthy as well as costly legal process. The New Jersey Supreme Court in effect told the Quinlans to continue in their own path of decision making.

This case outlines the two distinct roles of the next of kin and society at large in decisions concerning vital processes. Certainly the primary decision must rest with the next of kin -- in this case, the parents. Society's obligation is secondary: society should decide whether the parent's choice is a prudent one. The legal system should act as a reviewer of crucial decisions.

At this point, however, Karen Quinlan continues to be maintained by a respirator. If we are to take the court's recommendation seriously, then surely the Quinlan's decision should be carried out shortly, and Karen Quinlan should soon be allowed to die.

The National Catholic Reporter, May, 1976.

Note: Karen Quinlan eventually was weaned from her respirator. She died on June 11, 1985 after spending nine years in a New Jersey nursing home.

Mimeograph Mitosis

This story begins at the faculty mail boxes; it was at that location where I recently began erroneously to believe I had made an astounding biological discovery -- one that if true would have far-reaching consequences for cellular biology, theories of genetics and perhaps for the way stationery is bought and sold in this country.

It all began the other morning on my way up to the philosophy department on the fourth floor. While I waited patiently for the new elevator to whisk me away to the waiting work in my office (I think I was teaching that day about the problem of appearance and reality), I took a quick look in my faculty mailbox where I found one 8 1/2 by 11 inch sheet of white paper on which was mimeographed, in smelly purple ink, a smudged announcement of little or no importance. As I heard the bell for the elevator, I placed the paper back in my pigeon hole and proceeded to move on to loftier things.

On my way back from lunch, I was mulling over a particular student who had managed to present me with her own version of the problem of appearance and reality: she had propped her book on her desk so as to give the appearance of thinking diligently about the complicated matter at hand, while in reality sleeping away her philosophy class. I was forced out of my reverie, however, when I took another look in my mailbox and discovered it now mysteriously contained four pieces of white paper; each sheet was complete with its own announcement of little or no importance spelled out carefully in smudged-purple, mimeograph ink. At 2:30 I decided to ride the elevator to the book store which is situated in the basement just across from the faculty mail slots. By that time the number of mimeographed sheets resting comfortably in my box had increased to eight.

A few hours later, when I checked on my way home, there were sixteen sheets of various sizes, crammed, dog-eared in my pigeon hole. On the front of each sheet was a slightly different but nonetheless smelly and smudged announcement of little or no importance.

By the end of that day I had dimly begun to realize the interworkings of a complex and strange biological anomaly: mimeographed sheets of white paper on which are printed purple announcements of little or no importance reproduce themselves asexually but geometrically when left in an open-faced wooden container.

That very evening, the ramifications of this mysterious genetic discovery began to become clearer. It is amazing what the mind can do when it stops thinking about the problem of appearance and reality and begins instead to think about biological matters. In fact, it wasn't long before my mind began to swim with the possibilities of fame and fortune the revelation of this strange mimeograph mitosis might bring. In the late evening I dreamed Ted Koppel was asking me all sorts of very difficult questions about my discovery and whether I thought he looked like Alfred E. Newman. By the following morning, I began to work in earnest on a new, over-arching theory of genetics. I began to wonder if this principle of spontaneous generation might operate for any printed matter left in an open wooden container. (I had, for example, observed a similar pattern in regard to items sent to me by the publishers' clearing house and left in my postal box at home.)

But after placing my pay check in the same, small faculty box at about 10:00, by about 10:15 I had rather painfully discovered it is a phenomemon which seems solely to apply to mimeograph sheets bearing announcements of little or no importance. I did, however, discover a new principle of economics in the process of this biological experiment: it takes approximately 15 minutes for a faculty pay check to disappear when left in an open wooden container.

For the next several days, I was a little short of cash which provided me with ample time to carefully examine the exponential growth of mimeographed sheets bearing announcements of little or no importance. By the following Friday, I was ready to make some tentative but scholarly conclusions about my observations.

Before I made my discovery public, I called my friend in the biology department, a wise and energetic older nun. She answered my questions about the proper footnote form for papers bearing tentative but scholarly biological conclusions. But in the course of our conversation, I regrettably let slip the news of my breakthrough. She began to become suspicious, I think, when I asked her if she thought a potential Noble Prize winning scientist should wear a blue tie or a red tie with his grey suit if he were going to be on *Nightline*.

When the truth was finally out, she acted quite nonplused. Rather than enthusiastically embracing my new idea, and at the very least suggesting I send it to "Faculty Notes," a mimeographed sheet on which are copiously described professional activities of greater and lesser importance, she replied nonchalantly, "Oh, I've known that for years."

"Every evening, just after I put the frogs to bed over in the lab, I empty out all the faculty mailboxes of purple mimeographed sheets on which are printed announcements of little or no importance. Why do you think I became a member of the biology department? Lord knows where we would be in the morning if I hadn't."

Unpublished, Fall 1981.

*A*erial Criticism

For the past few years, I have been writing a rather long and laborious article entitled: "From Aristotle to Descartes: On Making Animals Anthropomorphic." It has grown to be a weighty tome, some 50 or so footnote filled pages, all devoted to the thesis that we tend to impute to animals human characteristics they do not actually possess.

I began writing the article at the urging of members of the education department at the National Zoo. For some time, they have expressed a concern that people who visit the zoo rarely see animals as they really are. Instead, they more often view them as human beings, trapped like so many unfortunate story book princes, in animal bodies. These misconceptions not only do a disservice to the animals, but they also may prevent people from fully enjoying the variety and mystery the animal world has to offer.

The article was completed some time ago, and I dutifully mailed it off to the publisher. It was with a certain sense of service and accomplishment I finished the task. It is always satisfying when philosophy can be taken out of the clouds and brought to bear in a practical way on some problem that relates to everyday life.

The other day, however, I'm afraid I received my first pre-publication criticism. It came from a disturbingly reliable source. While I was teaching the other morning, a pigeon flew in the open and screenless window of my office. He circled the room in a clockwise fashion, eventually landing on Cesaresco's *The Place of Animals in Human Thought*. The book, a turn of the century classic about the human propensity to endow animals with human characteristics, rests atop a pile of books and articles which served as the research materials for my paper. I know so much about the coming and going of the bird, for one of my students -- a bright and sensible young woman -- stood in the doorway of my office and watched incredulously as the pigeon lifted itself off the pile of scholarly materials and then carefully deposited a pile of unscholarly materials for which pigeons have become famous squarely in the middle of the red and gold cover of Cesaresco's monumental work.

With this task accomplished, the white and irridescent-purple visitor flew round the room a moment longer and then out the way it came, leaving his gastro-intestinal enigma to be pondered. I now must decide whether the aerial criticism was aimed at just Cesaresco's work, an admittedly outdated tract, or at some other particular book or article in the pile of materials, or, worse yet, at my scholarship as a whole.

I have spent the last several days feeling much like the shaman or medicine man of a primitive society who spends much of his time reading the entrails of pigeons in order to discern important truths about the nature and contours of reality. But there is a modern academic twist to the story. Unlike the medicine man I do not have access to the primary sources, the entrails themselves. Instead, I have been left, in typical scholarly fashion, with only the secondary sources, the by-product of the entrails. And it is from these secondary sources I must divine the significance of these events.

Whatever final interpretations I give to this episode, I was thinking about calling the folks at the National Zoo to tell them my paper may be in need of some revision. Somehow I feel like I have not included all that needs to be said about these matters.

🍂 Unpublished, Spring 1983.

*M*atters of the Heart

On the feast of St. Valentine, a second century martyr ironically known for his chastity and virtue, our thoughts turn to matters of the heart.

The heart: A one pound organ enclosed in a tough fibrous sac, the pericardium. It is shaped more or less like a pear, with the broad base formed by the two atria and the large vessels that enter and leave the heart like the entrance and exit ramps of a freeway. Between the fifth and sixth ribs, halfway across the left side of the chest, lies the apex, formed by the tip of the left ventrical. It looks a bit crooked, as it points downward and to the left. The front surface of the heart lies protected behind the oldest of battle armors, the sternum, and is formed by the right atria and right ventrical.

The heart: It begins to pulsate and move blood through the developing tissues of the body months before birth and continues unceasingly until death. Its total electrical output is about 2-1/2 watts, a fraction of that produced by the average household light bulb.

Yet, with the help of arteries, veins and capillaries, the rivers and smaller estuaries of the circulatory system, the heart is able to supply blood to even the most remote regions of the body. This pump, a little bigger than a clenched fist, circulates 300 quarts an hour, 1,800 gallons a day, 657,000 gallons a year, 46 million gallons in a lifetime.

Along the way, it beats relentlessly, about 70 times a minute, 40 million times a year, three billion beats per life, until ravages of time and gravitational pull put an end to the heroics of this remarkably efficient organ. The liquid legacy circulated through the body could fill a garden hose encircling the earth.

The heart: It has long had more than just functional significance. It has been identified with the very essence of humanity. Primitives often removed and ceremoniously ingested the hearts of newly dead shamans so that the power and knowledge of these holy men would remain a part of the culture. The Romans conceived of Cupid as a mischievous boy who could provoke both love and repulsion with his arrows aimed at the heart. The Roman appreciation for the importance of the heart can still be seen in certain English words pertaining to spirit and character such as "cordial" and "courage" which have their origins in cord, the Latin root for heart.

Blaise Pascal, the 16th century French philosopher, thought the heart had reasons that reason would never know -- that we could see it in a thousand ways. I think he was right.

Most of us live in our hearts. We break them and wear them on our sleeves. We have heart-to-heart talks and give hearty handshakes. We speak from the bottom of our hearts and give heartfelt thanks. We often feel our hearts in our throats or our mouths. We admire the young at heart. We hold special places in our hearts; we carry the dead around in them, each of us bearing his own private cemetery within.

But there is also that portion of the heart into which others may not enter, invite them as we may. It is here that our hearts magnify both their objects and themselves, regularly making unreasonable claims as to their own strength, duration and intensity. It is also in this secret place, this heart of hearts, where important changes of the heart take place. We move from being coldhearted to warmhearted, from hardhearted to softhearted.

But perhaps the biggest change of heart is yet to come. Some say this monumental change could bring a solution to the Tin Man's problem, though it might also aid Dorothy's tawny-coated friend, the Cowardly Lion, to move from being chicken-hearted to truly lion-hearted. Other less optimistic critics fear this new change may be the first step in making us all like tin men.

For the past 18 years federally funded research has been underway leading to the development and implantation of a totally synthetic, artificial heart. Until last year, this project, currently housed at the University of Utah Medical Center, received very little attention. Late in 1980, however, government permission was sought so that the center could begin to experiment with its device, using human subjects.

At present, the implanted pump the Utah group intends to use is pneumatically driven by two tubes that pass through the chest to an exterior power source. In the not-too-distant future, however, Dr. Robert Jarvik, the designer of the device, envisions an electrically driven artificial system, with the power coming from batteries worn on a belt and transmitted through a lead carrying a small cable through the skin. The cable would signal from a microcomputer, making the artificial heart patient totally mobile.

Dr. Jarvik recently commented on the goals of the Utah project in *Scientific American:* "If the artificial heart is ever to achieve its objective, it must be more than just a pump. It must also be more than just functional, reliable, and dependable. It must be forgettable."

Needless to say, there are many technical, legal and ethical problems which must be dealt with if we are ever to judge the artificial heart as a genuine step forward. A 1973 study of the synthetic heart program put the cost of a single operation at $50,000. At an annual inflation rate of 10 percent, who can afford $100,000 for a new ticker? Will artificial hearts continue to beat after brain and other vital organs cease to function? What moral and legal repercussions might the answer to this question have for current statutory definitions of death? Who will get these plastic pumps? What selection criteria should be used? Immediate need? First come first served? A lottery? Some measure of social worth? To whom should we entrust these important decisions?

More importantly, what philosophical, theological and psychological ramifications might the development and implantation of the artificial heart have for questions about the nature of self-identity?

When the natural heart, one of the central metaphors for courage, sensitivity and life itself, no longer occupies a key place in our social framework, what repercussions will it have for the ways in which we all see ourselves? What about the recipients? Will we succeed in making these people feel normal? Certainly if the new pump is effective, we may begin to see ourselves as conquerors of death, a kind of plasmal immortality in plastic. But might it also be the case that some of these people may feel dehumanized, empty-hearted, at the knowledge that their existence depends on just so much Dacron and electrical wire.

And so, in the not-too-distant future the feast of St. Valentine may still turn our thoughts to matters of the heart, but Cupid will be slinging wood and feathers at plexiglas and plastic, and reason will have invented a heart of which even Pascal's heart was entirely unaware.

Baltimore Sunday Sun, February, 1982.

The Baby Fae Case

There is a line in Friedrich Nietzsche's *Thus Spake Zarathustra* where he warns us to hold fast to our hearts, for when they fly, our heads often go with them. For the last several days the nation has watched as a heart was taken from the chest of a baboon and implanted in the body of a two-week-old infant. The resulting discussion of that procedure might lead the observer to believe that although it was the simian who has lost his heart it was humans who had lost their heads.

Most of the criticism that has surfaced about the Baby Fae case has come from animal rights groups who are displeased with the implantation of the animal heart because it not only sacrificed the life of the baboon, but it also caused useless suffering to the child. Other criticisms of the procedure seemed to have centered on the medical and ethical preferability of using the baboon heart as opposed to some other procedure. Some of the more important medical, ethical and social issues this case calls to mind, however, have yet to be discussed.

One of the principal issues underlined by the transplant is the sometimes foggy and ill-defined distinction in American medicine between experimentation and the practice of medicine. The difficulty inherent in distinguishing between these two elements of medicine is at least as old as the fifth century B.C. physician, Hippocrates, who informed us that while treating a boy whose cerebral cortex was exposed, he not only performed the necessary therapy, he also "gently scratched the cortex with [his] fingernail and observed convulsions on the other side of the body."

It has only been in the last century and a half that medicine has become aware of the need for deliberate, well-planned experimentation. The resulting role of the physician, since the time of Louis Pasteur, has often been one of the clinical researcher, as well as provider of professional care. At times these two different roles may pull the physician in opposite directions.

Because of the problems inherent with simultaneously performing both roles, most teaching hospitals in the United States have set up review boards to determine the ethical implications of experimental therapies. The primary purpose of these boards is to ensure that the proposed experimental treatment is undertaken with the proper informed consent of the patient, is done with full consideration of the rights and welfare of the patient, and is performed with an understanding of the risks and potential benefits of the therapy.

One important question to ask about the Baby Fae case is whether or not a more conventional treatment, such as the implantation of a human heart, was one of the available options in treating the child. The facts of the case seem very murky on this point. The attending physician. Dr. Leonard L. Bailey, admitted a few days after the transplant that the medical team had not sought a human organ donor. If a human heart was available for transplantation, it raises serious ethical questions about why the more proven procedure, the use of the human heart, was not deemed the preferred treatment.

A third issue this case calls to mind is, perhaps, the most important one. It can be raised in the form of a question: given limited medical resources, how much time, energy and money should be allocated for the prevention of heart disease and how much for what is sometimes called "rescue" or "crisis" medicine?

The answer to the question is clouded by insufficient care being given to the distinction between basic research and applied research. Some medical critics such as Ivan Illich in his

Medical Nemesis, claim that modern medicine is actually a threat to health for it drains away a good portion of funds allocated for health care by spending those monies on experimental therapies and very little on the prevention of disease.

Lewis Thomas, a respected member of the medical community, has responded by suggesting that we have not yet "begun modern medicine." It has only been since the invention of antibiotics in the 1940's that we have been able to cure a substantial number of diseases. Thomas argues that many diseases cannot be prevented because we do not sufficiently understand their mechanisms. Until we have more and better basic research, we will be forced to settle for what Thomas calls "half-way technologies."

These treatments, of which artificial and animal heart transplants are examples, are designed to compensate for the disease or postpone death. We treat the debilitating effects of heart disease without knowing enough about its structure and etiology. Thomas adds, "These half-way technologies are always very expensive and require elaborate facilities."

He urges that the medical community turn its attention toward a "high technology" approach to disease, one based on a thorough understanding of the origin and structure of disease. This approach, he suggests, would be simple and relatively inexpensive. For years, he adds, we continued with half-way treatments of polio with stop-gap measures like the iron lung, braces and other prosthetic devices. Jonas Salk finally took a simple and comparatively inexpensive approach with his development and introduction of the polio vaccine.

Many critics of the medical establishment have long been suggesting that the transplantation of organs, be they plastic, human or simian, should be abandoned in favor of more etiologically- and preventively-based research.

This proposal is, of course, at odds with the current public policy concerning the allocation of medical resources in this country. We spend approximately 12 percent of the federal budget each year on health care. In 1980 that figure, because of an annual medical inflation rate of 15 percent, had climbed to $250 billion.

If one examines the way those monies were assigned to the four major determinants of health care (biology, life-style, environment, and health-care systems) the results are striking. Over 90 percent of the $250 billion went to health care, 3 percent was allocated for the study of human biology, 1 percent went to life-style, and 5 percent to the study of the environment. Perhaps the most striking realization to be made about both the case of Baby Fae and that of Barney Clark, the first recipient of a totally artificial heart, is just how little attention we really spend on understanding the prevention of heart disease.

One final point Baby Fae's surgery calls to mind is one also shared by those who reflect on the implanting of Barney Clark's plastic heart. In both these cases it is clear some of the criticism come from a psychological rather than medical or ethical source. Throughout Western history the heart has carried with it a host of emotional and spiritual connotations -- connotations we do not want so easily to give up. Nietzsche says when we lose our hearts our heads follow. Even the most scientific and rational of us must stop, at least for a moment, to wonder if it is just our heads we lose.

Baltimore Evening Sun, November, 1984.

Note: Baby Fae died on November 15, 1984.

The Mary Robaczynski Case

> Caesar: Of all the wonders that I have yet heard, it seems to me most strange that men should fear; seeing that death, a necessary end, will come when it will come.
>
> *--Julius Caesar* II 2

The trial of Mary Rose Robaczynski ended last week; the jury was unable to decide unanimously on her guilt or innocence. The trial provided a few surprises. To me the biggest one, probably due to my naivete about the law, was that it produced so much discussion about the legal issues involved, and little else, the principle legal question being, was Harry Gessner alive or dead when Mrs. Robaczynski disconnected his respirator in the early morning of March 8, 1978?

During the course of the trial, the prosecution and the defense tried to answer this question. Each arrived at a different conclusion, though each has used the same criteria -- that contained in the Maryland statutory definition of death.

When any issue other than this succinct legal one was raised, objections from both sides of the aisle were voiced. In these instances Judge Robert Karwacki, probably realizing the difficulties that might invest the trial were complicated philosophical questions added to the already confusing testimony, invariably sustained these objections. Even in summation both sides chose to avoid ethical discussion in favor of arguing more the narrow question of whether Mr. Gessner was alive or dead, according to Maryland law.

Yet, conversations heard both in and outside the court building during and after the trial were seldom about this narrow legal issue. Most were about the larger questions the trial provoked--questions that cross the disciplines of biology, sociology, philosophy and medicine.

Of course the state's legal definition of death is of itself important. This statute says, in part, that pronoucements of death "shall be based on ordinary standards of medical practice." For most contemporary physicians these "ordinary standards" have become synonymous with the criteria developed by an *ad hoc* committee of the Harvard Medical School. These standards consist of four parts: first, a lack of spontaneous breathing; second, fixed and dilated pupils; third, no response to external stimuli; and finally, an absence of brain activity as displayed on an electroencephalogram. This fourth criterion was thought by the committee to be the strongest confirmation.

These criteria were developed, among other reasons, to clear up some confusion surrounding the previous "vital signs" definition. In 1958, the Supreme Court of Arkansas decided a case in which a husband and wife were involved in an automobile accident. The husband died instantly. His wife was taken to the hospital unconscious. It was alleged by the petitioner, the couples' heir, that "she remained in a coma due to brain injury," in effect trying to argue that they had died simultaneously. Implicit in this argument was the notion that "life" should be associated with brain activity.

The Harvard committee was certain that its new definition would go a long way toward clearing up the definitional problem raised in this case, as well as similar cases in California and Virginia. A short time later, Kansas, Michigan, Oregon, California, Virginia, Georgia, New Mexico and Maryland had all developed statutory definitions of death, patterned on the Harvard criteria.

When "brain activity" is mentioned in the Harvard standards it refers to any activity that can be registered on the EEG. Because of this interpretation, there is an increasing disagreement among physicians and ethicists on these criteria. Robert Veatch in his book, *Death, Dying, and the Biological Revolution*, argues that irreversible loss of functioning in the cerebral neocortex, the place where a higher brain activity takes place, rather than the whole brain, ought to be the fundamental determinant of death. Indeed he sees the more conventional criteria (which were applied to Harry Gessner), spinal and brainstem reflexes, as largely irrelevant to the determination of death.

A second issue related to this initial one is the question of whether in cases such as Mr. Gessner's we are prolonging life or extending the process of dying. With modern medical techniques, apparatus and drugs, to keep alive people who are *in extremis*. Traditional moralists often draw a distinction between "ordinary" and "extraordinary" medical or surgical procedures in regard to patients of this kind. "Ordinary" measures were thought to include any treatment a patient could obtain without causing an undue burden to himself or to his family. "Extraordinary" treatment usually has been conceived as that which is "costly, extremely painful, very difficult or dangerous."

Unfortunately, this reasonably clear distinction does not fit people like Harry Gessner. Many of the mechanical procedures now in use originally were invented as temporary means for aiding the patient, their purpose being to win time for the restoration process to take place. If this purpose has not been achieved in a reasonable length of time, it may be said that these devices have failed.

Have we developed the respirator for the purpose of creating a population of patients, perhaps as many as one million in the

United States, who are in a condition of artificially arrested death? We must remember that the Hippocratic oath was not written in an era of the Monaghan Series 200 respirator. Yet, there is a general attitude in the medical profession that any death is a defeat, that responsible patient care dictates the use of every conceivable device and strategem. In the meantime, the families of these patients are often footing the bills.

These considerations lead us to a third issue the trial calls to mind: In the absence of consciousness on the part of the patient, who makes decisions to terminate or extend treatment? Traditionally in our society when a person is incapable of speaking for himself, that duty usually passes to the next of kin. During the entire two weeks of testimony no mention was made of Mr. Gessner's brother or sisters who visited him daily in the hospital.

A final issue to be raised about the ramifications of this case returns us to our starting point, the law. Cases like Mary Robaczynski's are an indication of a changing legal climate in terms of the practice of medicine and an ever-increasing concern for the protection of the patient in American jurisprudence. The rising incidence of malpractice suits is thought by many physicians to create a handicap which not only undermines the trust of the patient, but also limits the physician in terms of what should be his primary responsibility, the welfare of the patient.

Needless to say, all of these issues are very important. The case exemplifies how far we have come from a time in which a mirror was held to the nostrils of Cordelia to see if she was dead. But it also burdens us with a new responsibility -- one that must be shared if we are to use technology wisely.

Baltimore Sunday Sun, March, 1979.

*P*sychologist at Work

The other afternoon, while meandering along the main street of this small Scottish town, I happened upon my friend Charles, the psychologist. He was standing on the corner, clipboard in hand, accompanied by another psychologist similarly equipped. They both stood intently staring across the street at the outdoor bank machine where an elderly woman with two enormous shopping bags was busy making a transaction.

As I approached, I inquired as to Charles' health (a momentary and inexplicable loss of long-term memory prohibited me from recalling what an extended discourse a question of this nature is likely to evoke when asked of a psychologist.) Only later, after a bit of reflection did his response surprise me, for he said that he was fine but could not talk to me now because, as he put it, he was working. I looked around South Street for the rats with electrodes attached to their heads who usually accompany Charles when he is working, but they were nowhere to be found.

During my brief search, Charles and his companion, a bespectacled younger man who looked like the one kid in every 1960's American High school class who always carried a slide-rule on his belt, had the following conversation:

Charles: *She gets two for head-turning.*

Second psychologist:
(excitedly) Yes, yes, and one for body-orientation posturing behavior.

Charles: *(more excitedly) Will you look at that cash-withdrawal transaction behavior?*

Second psychologist:
Yes! A bona-fide plus two.

With that, an armored truck, bearing the unmistakable logo of the bank, pulled round the corner and parked squarely in front of the building, completely obscuring the psychologists' view of the bank machine.

Second psychologist:
> *(dejectedly) Oh look at that, they've ruined our experiment. We're going to have to change our M.T.B.A.P.*

Vicchio: *(inquisitively) Charles, what's an M.T.B.A.P.?*

Charles: *Stephen ... can't you see I'm working here? ... Why it's ... it's Monitoring Transaction Behavior Analysis Position. It's where we stand to watch people use the bank machine. Really ... you're adding another variable to our analysis.*

Second psychologist:
> *(angrily) Yes, you're introducing noise in our sample.*

Now I have always prided myself on knowing when I am in danger of adding noise to someone's sample, so I was not at all put off by the insinuation that I had become an unwanted variable. Consequently, I resumed my sojourn along South Street, with its cobblestones and small shops. As I did, however, I could not help but recall how often my psychologist friends have told me they are on what they call "the cutting edge of science." Psychology has come a long way, they forcefully insist, since Pavlov's dogs, Freud's melancholics and Jung's collective unconscious.

Still, no matter how hard I tried I could not imagine Sigmund Freud, cigar in mouth, Professor Fliess by his side, watching an elderly woman press the little red buttons on a bank machine. But then, later in the evening, I was forced to rethink my position. I was preparing for bed, and as I crawled between the sheets, I picked up my copy of the Freud-Jung correspondence from the night table and mysteriously opened to a letter dated April 13, 1924.

Sehr geehrter Herr professor:

Ich weiss, wie enttauscht sie uber meine Arbeit sind seit unserem bruch. Ich glaube aber jetzt im begriff zu sein, etwas tatsachlich neues zu entdecken. Heute morgen, wahrend eines entscheidenden Experiments, war ich gerade am rande eines durchbruchs, als mir ein Pferdefuhrwerk die Sicht auf mein Untersuchungsobjekt, eine Lebensmittelhandlung, versperrte. In der hoffnung Ihnen bald neues mitteilen zu konnen verbleibe ich als Ihr ergebener Schuler.

Carl Gustav

I was so surprised, it was several hours before I had managed a clear translation:

My Dear professor:

I know how disappointed you are with my work since our split, but I think I am truly on to something now. This morning during a crucial experiment I was on the verge of a breakthrough but a horse-drawn carriage parked in front of the general store.

Your Student,

Carl Gustav

When I finally got to sleep in the early hours of that morning, it was with a heavy conscience. I made a promise to myself to never again bother Charles when he is working. I don't wish to be noise in anyone's sample.

Baltimore Evening Sun, June, 1984.

Of Plastic Hearts

On June 3, 1965 millions of hopeful Americans, as well as the rest of the world, watched flickering television pictures of Edward H. White as he gingerly, excited from his Gemini IV space craft, and, while connected to the ship by an unbilical cord, began a historic walk in space.

On December 2, 1982, shortly after midnight, a 61-year-old retired dentist, Barney B. Clark, although lying motionless and anesthesized on an operating table at the University of Utah Medical Center, became the first of what surely is to become a new kind of pioneer, embarking on another uncharted, technological frontier, as promising as the Gemini flight, and just as forboding; he had become the first of what is perhaps a new race of Prometheuses, cursing the gods and living in plastic to tell about it. Clark has been hooked by twin, six-foot tether lines to a 375-pound air compressor which rhythmically and methodically began to drive a two-pound, pale yellow, artificial heart implanted in his chest.

The operation, a 7-1/2 hour miracle in polyurethane and aluminum, was pronounced a guarded success by Dr. William De Vries, the head of the surgical team. The historic implantation of the device was the culmination of a collective effort which saw the expenditure of $161 million in research funds and 16 years of intensive development of the Jarvik-7 and its six progenitors.

This event is surely one of the most monumental feats in the history of medicine. Our hopes go with Clark as we cheer him and his performance of ordinarily simple activities like the dangling of his feet over the side of a hospital bed. But there are still observations to be made here and questions to be raised that go beyond our human care for Barney Clark.

This operation calls to mind a myriad of issues worth remembering and also begs for certain questions to be raised -- questions about whether Clark will ultimately be seen as a hero or as the first in a long line of bionic Fausts. These larger questions are surely worth asking, even if they are not now answerable.

One thought the historic implantation calls to mind is that the man by the swimming pool in the movie *The Graduate* who gave Benjamin that one word of advice about the future: "plastics," may not have been far wrong. Spare parts for the human body have become a reality in the decade and a half since *The Graduate*. Most of the successes to date have come in the area of arthroscopy, with artificial substitutes now available for all the major appendages. We can now also overhaul arteries in Dacron and Teflon, urinary sphincters in silicone and rubber, middle ear stapes of Teflon and tantalum wire, and eustachian tubes and artificial lungs in silastic.

Patients are now currently wearing portable, battery-operated, artificial kidneys developed at the University of Utah Medical Center. Great advances have also been made in the past decade in the development of an artificial pancreas which could eliminate the long-term complications of diabetes. Similar gains have been made in artificial liver research. Artificial whole blood and intervertebral discs of Silicone and Dacron are now a reality. Artificial ligaments, tendons and muscles are no longer to be found just in Mary Shelly and reruns of the *The Six Million Dollar Man*.

Although spare parts medicine has been at least an embryonic reality since the late 1960's, it is significant that it has captured the imagination of Americans now with the first permanent implantation of an artificial heart. It may tell us something about just how carefully we still identify the heart as the seat of emotions and sensitivity. It also surely has something to do with the fact is the nation's number one killer, claiming 700,000 annually.

This brings us to another notion that Clark's surgery calls to mind: In the last several decades the pattern of disease in this country has changed rapidly and drastically. Our grandparents generation was plagued by infections. Consequently, they lived relatively short lives. We live much longer today, usually succumbing to 70 years of gravitational pull on our hearts, or to cancer. People stopped dying of infections in this country because of medical gains made by relatively cheap means: vaccination, mass immunization and the development of antibiotics.

One point that the dramatic implantation of the artificial heart calls to mind is that the prevention of death by these two new killers, heart disease and cancer, demands much more highly specialized treatments, with much more sophisticated equipment and technical expertise. The story of Clark highlights this fact but there are also hundreds of thousands of people, with admittedly less spectacular and less expensive but still quite costly kinds of procedures and therapies, who give testimony to just how expensive it is going to be in the future to treat diseases which our grandparents did not live long enough to contract.

The initial cost of Clark's operation has been estimated at $75,000, with annual expenses of several thousand dollars a year for maintenance. If and when these plastic hearts become available to a larger number of the public who need them, who will pay for them? Will the government foot the bill, particularly now when various agencies seem to be routinely cutting back on social services and medical benefits? Insurance companies may be very reluctant to cover the cost without consumers paying considerably higher premiums. If the government and insurance companies do not assume the cost then these hearts will, practically speaking, only be available to those who can afford them. This situation calls to mind the crippled man in the *Gospel of John* who lay helplessly beside a healing pool while he waited in vain for someone to lift him in the water.

Another set of issues, perhaps more important, but equally as complex, are broader range ethical and social ones. In these radically new procedures what does "informed consent" amount to? In Clark's case the choice seemed relatively clear. If he had not chosen the implantation, he would have been dead in a very short time. But there are cases on the horizon where the ethical choices may be much harder than this one.

In an area so fraught with emotions, what provisions will be made for the psychological and emotional repercussions of living with artificial, but vital, organs? Dr. Clark has been given a key to his heart; he has the ability to turn the device off at any point. Will we provide heart recipients of the future with this option? Why did we do it with the first?

Another far reaching question involves just how far we can go with spare parts medicine. What about the brain? What makes a human being a human being? It reminds one of the old philosophical problem of the man who changed a few different planks of his small boat every spring until, several years later, he had a whole new boat. At what point do I become a whole new me? Am I me so long as I have the same memories, though I may have a different body? In the *Aeneid* Virgil comments: "They can because they know they can." This may be the motto for much of modern medicine.

In the *Wizard of Oz* the old man complies with the Tin Man's request for a new heart by handing him an oversized watch. In Utah we may have taken the first step in really solving the Tin

Man's problem. But it may also be the case that unless we continue to ask the right questions about what we are doing, it may be the first step in turning us all into tin men.

                         Baltimore Evening Sun, January, 1983.

Note: Barney Clark died on March 23, 1983.

ACADEMIA

*The whole drift of my education
goes to persuade me that the world of our present
consciousness in only one out of many worlds
of consciousness that exist.*

🍎 *-- William James*

Epitaph For a Teacher

> I was, but am no more, thank God -- a school teacher -- I dreamed last night I was teaching again -- that's the only bad dream that ever afflicts my sturdy conscience.
> --D.H. Lawrence

> Benevolence alone will not make a teacher, nor will learning alone do it. The gift of teaching is a peculiar talent, and implies a need and a craving in the teacher himself.
> --John Jay Chapman

Teaching. It is a profession that more resembles dentistry and marathon running than anything else. This point should be made more clearly; not dentistry or marathon running, dentistry and marathon running -- the conjunction is very important. Teaching is essentially like pulling teeth, while in the midst of running flat-out for 26 miles 385 yards. It is not the sort of thing most normal people want to do.

Because being a teacher is very difficult, and because it does not pay very well, there are very few good ones. But even the best teachers, toward the end of May, begin to exhibit that characteristically haggard look of the dental marathoner. The only real problem with this analogy is that in a peculiar kind of way it is the doctor who inevitably feels the pain of extraction, not the patient.

One of the biggest problems with the practice of dental marathoning is that it becomes more difficult, as the year rolls on, to deal with adversity. A broken ditto machine in September is a minor annoyance. In May it may well be the cause of the finding of the body of a Gestetner repairman on the floor of the faculty duplicating room.

The experienced teacher knows that by late April the practice of dental marathoning seems often to feel more like it is done with a 14-cubic-foot refrigerator strapped to one's back. It is not made any easier by listening to parents, who would never for a moment think about encouraging their children to consider the teaching profession, suggesting that education is the greatest and noblest of human callings.

It became even more difficult the other day while sitting in a faculty meeting. After listening to a short proposal concerning a new program in the humanities, a colleague turned to the rest of the committee and said, "We have heard a lot of ideas here today - about justice and beauty and truth -- but what does this have to do with the real world?"

It is difficult to explain while balancing a 14-cubic-foot refrigerator on one's back, that ideas are the real world. It took me a couple of days to recover from that encounter. Eventually, I chalked it up to the fact that at the time of my colleague's question he had his own refrigerator full of ideas to bear -- the strain was apparently too much for him.

Yesterday, however, I had another experience which may yet prove to be fatal. In an article in our college newspaper a student studying marketing was quoted as saying the humanities, as well as the Judeo-Christian heritage, were honorable, but not profitable.

After reading that quotation, for the better part of the evening I envisioned my grave-site -- neatly trimmed green grass on which sat a refrigerator-shaped tombstone with running shoes and dental tools emblazoned on the top. Underneath could be found the epitaph:

Stephen Vicchio
Honorable but not Profitable

When I arrived at the college this morning I was ready to give my scheduled examination and then lie down and die. I reached into my bookshelf, however, and found a graduation address given in 1955 by Adlai Stevenson at Smith College. He began that address, exactly 30 years ago, with these words:

> "The typical Western man...operates well in the realm of means, as the Romans did before him. But outside his specialty, in the realm of ends he is apt to operate poorly or not at all....The neglect of the cultivation of more mature values can only mean that his life, and the life of the society he determines, will lack vivid purpose, however busy and even profitable it may be."

I sat for a few moments at my desk. Finally, I took these words and put them into my refrigerator, knowing they will only make it heavier. I strapped the huge box to my back, grabbed up my running shoes and dental instruments. The end of the term is not far away.

Baltimore Evening Sun, May, 1985.

*T*erminal Case of Love

Professor S.J. Sisyphus opened the door to this office with great trepidation. The source of his uneasiness was not the darkness of the deserted hallway leading to the philosophy department, nor was it the lateness of the hour. The anxiety he was feeling had its origin in the fact that he had not seen his typewriter for months. He was not at all certain what the encounter with the worn Smith-Corona might bring.

In the last few weeks of a waning summer he had taken up with a word processor. And oh what a word processor it was. It was sleek and classy, with all its drive belts in the right places. In the beginning it was all fun and games, but lately it had gotten very serious. Things were made more complicated by his longstanding relationship with the now old, but still reliable, electric typewriter. He had returned to his office to write some letters on the worn machine. He was not sure how he or the typewriter would handle the delicate situation.

As the professor blew the dust from the neglected keys, he could feel a certain tightness in his throat. He flicked the switch to the "on" position, and settled uneasily into the creaking swivel chair. After adjusting the paper, his finger tips cautiously moved the keys for "Dear Morris." But rather than the paper displaying a salutation to his old college roommate, the keys mysteriously began to depress themselves. After a few clicks and clacks, the message on the white bond paper read:

"Where have you been? You think you can waltz right in here, after not seeing me for months, and put your hands all over me?"

Dr. Sisyphus fumbled for a moment. He glanced away from the keyboard. "Well," he stammered apologetically, "I've been working late in the computer center and I lost track of the ..."

The neglected machine shot back instantly, as if it had anticipated the professor's story:

"I know very well where you have been...You use me for all those years, the best years of my life, and now the first time you spot a hot little number with a little live current running through her, you become Mr. User Friendly."

The professor could feel the flush of embarrassment rising in his cheeks. "No, its not like that at all," he responded sheepishly, "we have been working together on an important paper on Rene Descartes."

"Don't lie to me, you ungrateful lout. You must think I was manufactured yesterday."

Sisyphus' trembling fingers moved for the "off" switch. In that instant he thought of the beginning of their relationship, how they had done everything together -- essays, book reviews, poetry. Back then, the Smith-Corona was responsive to his every touch. But now the electricity had gone out of their relationship.

"Yeah, that's the easy way out. You don't want to hear what I have to say. Well Buster, you seem conveniently to forget things. Who helped you through graduate school? And who typed that boring dissertation on "Wittgenstein and the Existence of Other Minds?" Now you're a big man and you don't need me hanging around anymore?"

Sisyphus knew his typewriter was right. At a deeper level he also understood many men his age have made the same mistake -- their eyes begin to wander. There was his friend Fred, a member of the geology department. He had abandoned his typewriter completely. He came into his office one morning and moved the Olivetti out. Lately he had taken to wearing leisure suits and a miniature floppy disc on a gold chain around his neck. He could be found hanging around the computer center until all hours of the morning.

After a moment of hesitation -- a moment in which he thought of how young the word processor had made him feel -- he got down on his knees and pledged to his typewriter they would make a new start.

The silence which followed seemed to the professor like an eternity. Finally, there could be heard the familiar clicks and clacks:

"I love you very much and I am willing to forgive and forget. Unlike that voltaic hussy you've been chasing, I have not been equipped with a 15K memory."

Baltimore Evening Sun, October, 1985.

Camus' Philosophy: *VARROOOM!*

I am slowly becoming aware of the inescapability of the use of audio-visual aids in the craft of teaching. It is not an awareness that has come over me all at once, it is something I have only begun to comprehend over time.

The other day while I stood before an eager summer class and as we discussed the concept of "the absurd life" in Albert Camus' novel, *The Stranger,* outside a little man seated astride a gigantic tractor roared up to a very small but placid patch of green grass. He wore a pair of orange industrial strength ear muffs, presumably to keep him from going deaf or crazy while accomplishing his task.

In a few moments, over the din of the tractor's vibrating innards, but in the direction of my students whose teeth were involuntarily chattering in synch with the firing of the tractor's pistons, I began to scream a whole series of observations like: 'WE MUST BEGIN TO APPRECIATE THE SPECIAL UNDERSTANDING CAMUS HAS FOR THE INCONGRUITIES OF LIFE." To the students, it sounded more like: "We must VAAAROOOOOM to VAAROOOMingROOM-ROOM ROOMROOM of life."

After a short while, I stopped. Sisyphus had rolled the rock one too many times. I looked out in the direction of the patch of land. In the corner of the window frame a spider was oscillating violently while trying to spin his silken web. Beyond the distressed spider sat the little man. He sensed my presence. While keeping one hand firmly on the wheel (he had to be careful not to run into the statue of the Blessed Mother in the center of the plot), he gave me a little wave. In the process of executing that gesture, he also flashed a rather serene, or perhaps knowing smile.

The smile, I now believe, is related to the fact that without my knowledge the dean has assigned this man to be the permanent audio-visual aid for my classes. That is the only explanation I can muster for why this man has been following me around.

In the autumn term, just after handing my detailed syllabi in to the dean's office, the leaves had begun to make their mournful descent to earth. Before long, the little man could be found, outside my classroom window, decked out in overalls, industrial strength ear muffs, and knowing smile. His hands gripped a small, box-shaped machine which resembled the body of a Texas chain saw, without the blade. In its place was a long rubber anteater's snout.

In class, as I began to discuss the dangers of an ever-encroaching technology, outside, with the help of the long-nosed box, the man was in the process of WHINING and WHOOSHING the leaves into order. Indeed, he seemed to WHINE and WHOOSH that same pile of leaves in and out of order for the next several months. (I might hasten to add the college does not own a rake. A rake does not operate on gasoline or electricity and doesn't WHINE or WHOOSH nearly enough to be an audio-visual aid.)

At the first sign of snow, the little man replaced the orange leaf-blowing snout with a black, snow-blowing snout. By then, we were discussing in my philosophy of art class the importance of the concept of perfect pitch. For the next several weeks, the little man proceeded to blow snow on and off the sidewalk just outside my classroom. He did it in the key of C.

Periodically, he would look up from his performance and give me that little wave and knowing smile.

In the spring, he put the exhausted little machine to rest and rolled out the gigantic tractor. Since early April, he has been cutting and recutting the grass just outside my classroom window. This will continue, presumably, until I die of hay fever or one of my students thoughtfully screams over the roar of the tractor, "You know, professor, we must VAAROOOOO to VAA-ROOOMing ROOMROOMROOMROOM of life."

🌰   *Baltimore Evening Sun,* June, 1985.

*M*ay's End

> He is either dead or teaching school
> --Zenobius (1st century B.C.)

The end of every May brings with it a certain recognizable depression: it is usually accompanied by a worn-out feeling and the vague but nonetheless real sensation that I have once again been a failure at something terribly important. The school year takes its toll.

Perhaps some of the uneasiness can be attributed to the time of the year set aside for formal teaching and learning. It has always seemed to me such an unnatural thing. We begin in the late summer in what Thomas Wolf calls "a season of sadness and departure." While drifting yellow leaves signal the natural world is coming to a close, teachers meet a new group of energetic, wide-eyed students and embark together on a journey we hope will not just load their minds, but will also enlarge them. Those of us who teach each year set out on that voyage with the firm conviction it can be done better this time. We can be clearer, more patient, better organized. We can overcome our shortcomings from the year before.

By late May, the journey has ended. It comes to a close when, as Rilke says, "Things are blooming recklessly." We ask our students to concentrate on final exams while outside the classroom flowers blaze as though wired by some Divine Electrician. Inside, teachers and students alike drag themselves through the final days of school. Students see the last day as escape, or at the very least, as release. Teachers see students as jumping ship before the job is ever finished.

I never remember a time when, by the end of the year, I firmly believed I had fully accomplished what I set out to do. There is always a lack of clarity on my part, too many loose ends, too many students unreached, too much time misplaced or ill-spent.

There is also, by the final exam, the nagging impression that some of my students feel that all semester I have passed on dead knowledge, embalmed in some slightly older form than it was passed on to me. This time of year, I am always reminded of the student who raised her hand rather petulantly and asked. "Are we only going to study dead people in this class?" You can see it in their eyes. They often appear to feel sorry for me. They usually sit far to the back of the room. They often speak to each other in hushed tones, as though they have been mistakenly invited to the funeral of someone they hardly knew.

All term, I have tried to give them some hint the material has been assimilated by me -- that I have read my own experiences into it. I have attempted to show what I teach has come to mean something more to me than a duty to pass on complicated and irrelevant messages from the past. By the end of May, it is clear I once again have been less than successful.

But this year, the accompanying depression seems less intense. I suspect it has something to do with a phone conversation I had the other evening with my mentor from graduate school. He is a man who for the last 40 years has dedicated his life to writing and teaching. During the course of our conversation, he asked how I was managing so close to the end of another school year. In a few short declarative sentences I voiced my concern about the students I had not reached, about all I once again had not accomplished.

"I have come to realize," he finally responded, "the aim of good teaching is to fail a little more nobly the next time."

This year, in late May, I have come to realize he is right.

Baltimore Evening Sun, May, 1986.

*T*ake a Philosopher to Lunch

Recently, I found myself at a rather large dinner party -- the kind where each place setting has more forks than the entire collection in my kitchen utensil drawer. I used to manage reasonably well at these affairs, due in large measure to some advice my mother gave me long ago when she feared I might some day be invited to gatherings such as this: start on the outside and work your way in. A few years ago, however, I began to be asked to a somewhat more elegant *soirée,* complete with tiny little forks at the head of each plate. The sight of these extra implements soon began to induce in me a kind of paralysis unknown to the Vanderbilts. Even they, of course start on the outside and work their way in, at least as far as forks are concerned, but they never find themselves in that position socially.

The fates, or perhaps it was simply the hostess's meticulously crafted seating plan, had preordained that I be placed next to an elderly and exceedingly dignified looking lady. Her flawlessly arranged hair, defying at least one of Newton's laws, and her clear, bright eyes, were of approximately the same shade of pale blue. Those eyes, or perhaps it was the coiffure, put me in the mind of that rather large, aquamarine wave that relentlessly pounds the beach at the beginning of *Hawaii Five-0* reruns, except here, on her head, the wave was frozen, protruding conspiciously from the side of her face, stuck in some strange aquatic time warp.

Initially, I thought perhaps it was due to my impolitely fixing a gaze at her immutable turquoise ripple that for the next several hours the woman repeatedly spurned all of my half-hearted attempts at polite dinner party conversation. But then, later in the meal, the truth reared its ugly head. All at once this refined octogenarian turned to me and muttered in a voice more than a bit reminiscent of Perry Mason's perpetually defeated nemesis, Hamilton Burger, "So, you are a philosopher!"

I felt my face turn the color of summer beets. "No", I fumbled apologetically, "I just teach philosophy." But somehow my disclaimer fell limply into the *pommes de terre*. She drew back and stared at me with thinly veiled but nonetheless unmistakable disapproval. "Well," she intoned reproachfully, "you are far too young to be so resigned."

Still later, some time between the Spanish melon and the Colombian coffee, I realized it had happened again. This noble Roland Park matron hadn't an inkling as to what philosophy is or does.

For those Americans who don't regularly confuse philosophy for psychology (many of my distant relations have over the last few years inquired as to the availability of free psychiatric counseling), the craft of Plato, Pascal and Popper is seen as a kind of passive contemplation, usually conducted in impotence -- private consolation for public failure. In America we exhort people to take things "philosophically," which cashes out to mean a kind of resignation only properly attributed to the deeply comatose and the dead.

This summer, a colleague of mine, a theology professor, went to a teaching workshop, where he was afforded the opportunity of enlisting the aid of a computer in constructing a list of instructional materials for use in his classes. When he plugged the word "theology" into the voltaic brain, he received a readout resembling the white runner in the center aisle of an Episcopal wedding. When he tried "philosophy", the display screen read: "Does Not Compute". If only philosophers had angels they could count dancing on the heads of pins.

A few months ago, a friend of mine, an unemployed philosophy teacher (he's taking it philosophically), attempted to collect unemployment compensation. His interview was going just splendidly until he was asked his occupation. "Philosopher," my friend responded quite matter-of-factly. "Yeah, sure," the interviewer shot back, "We're all philosophers here, but what the hell do you do for a living?" Had the instructor assured the official that he was a brain surgeon, the interviewer might have wondered why the applicant was without work in a culture such as ours, but he would not have been tempted to say, "Sure, we're all brain surgeons." Ironically enough, it took my chum just as long to learn the craft of philosophy as it does others to master the intricacies of neurosurgery. And doing philosophy poorly can destroy a good idea just as surely as an inept physician can kill a patient.

Had my dignified dinner companion given me the chance, I might have tried to discuss with her what I do think philosophy is, and why I think it is an essential discipline. But the opportunity did not present itself. The conversation headed off in a direction where it would have seemed quite unnatural to interject several paragraphs on the nature and function of Aristotle's enterprise.

And so, after some thought, I have decided to declare the month of August "Take a Philosopher to Lunch Month." You can obtain the number of the department of philosophy at your nearest college or university by dialing the information number of the school. Within the confines of a small, intimate restaurant, you could ask your designated philosopher about his area of specialization, or perhaps how he or she feels about the mind/body problem, the existence of other minds, or arguments for the existence of the material world, something that will come in handy when the check arrives. But above all, don't take your philosopher to those places where you will find those tiny little forks at the top of each place setting. They sometimes get terribly disoriented.

Baltimore Evening Sun, July, 1983.

Grad Speaker Available

This is about a graduation address no one has asked me to give. I've been all dressed up, with commencement address in hand, and no place to go. I did deliver a graduation talk last year. I thought it was very good, which is why I am a bit surprised and hurt I'm not booked up this spring.

In last year's talk, I told the graduates they would be the leaders of tomorrow and they stood at a crucial crossroads in history -- a time never before seen by human kind. A few weeks later, while reading *Time,* I discovered Edward Kennedy and Garry Wills had said exactly the same things to groups of graduates in New Haven, Connecuticut, and Cambridge, Massachusetts, and I wasn't even offended, though I had made my remarks a full 48 hours before either one of them.

This year, in anticipation of an overwhelming number of solicitations for my services, I spent several weeks preparing my new talk. It is all about education and closing the windows of vulnerability. But alas, the invitations did not come. I've been waiting here by the faculty mailboxes, dressed in my academic regalia, for the last several weeks.

For a few days in early May I even held my classes in the mail room. While we discussed what is truth and the existence of God, I always kept an eye peeled for the red, white and blue truck with the steering wheel on the wrong side driven by the guy with the short grey pants, blue knee highs and the dog mace attached to his pith helmet.

I began to figure that an entire year is enough time for the news of just how good I was last year to disseminate to those small colleges and universities in the outlying areas still lacking a distinguished graduation speaker.

I almost had an engagement at a local Catholic high school. But while the president of the senior class was assuring me how philosophically minded all the gang in the commercial course are, the principal, apparently a man of more pragmatic wisdom, had engaged the services of the Tactical Commander of the Baltimore County SWAT team to deliver the address.

As luck would have it, the commander had also given a graduation talk last year. It was a combination fire arms display and commencement address at a local Quaker school. And since word has it that he received a standing ovation, he seems this year to have guaranteed his appearance at the parochial school's podium.

Finally, toward the end of the last week, as I was beginning to contemplate the packing up of my mortar board and academic hood, I got a call from the Precocious Pup Canine College, a local obedience school. It seems their graduation speaker had come down with a bit of distemper, and the president of the school, after informing me of all the wonderful things he had heard about my last year's address, inquired as to my availability later that afternoon.

I had him wait on the line while I checked my "busy graduation calendar." In a moment I returned to the phone and, while I had the guys in the mail room rustle paper in the background and shout how busy it was around there this time of year, I informed him that there had been a late cancellation and that I thought I could fit him in.

That morning I immediately went to work on a talk on "Housebreaking Your Pet and the Window of Vulnerability." Unfortunately, the engagement was a disaster. Many of the dogs dozed off and a very curt older woman with a shitzu under her arm informed me afterwards that she now understood the definition of a college professor: "someone who talks in other people's sleep."

Immanuel Kant once remarked that "Metaphysics is a dark ocean without shores or lighthouses, strewn with many a philosophical wreck." I wonder if he ever gave a graduation address at a dog obedience school?

🍎 *Baltimore Evening Sun,* May, 1983.

Scatology and Eschatology

I am living in the middle of a Borges short story -- one of those mysterious tales about love and death, the mind of God, or the dual illusions of time and eternity. It all began a few weeks ago when our bathtub disappeared. There were no witnesses. The police refused to take a statement. They referred my complaint to the department of water and sewerage.

The tub in question used to rest on four of those wonderful, Victorian cast-iron feet in the faculty rest room just a few paces from my office in the philosophy department. They (the feet) were securely connected to the porcelain body of the tub last Wednesday when I left my office. Thursday morning, the whole thing was gone.

When as a child I used to regularly lose my shoes before school, my mother would inform me in quite reproachful tones, that not only did she not wear them, but also they did not just walk away. Now, many years later, I'm not so sure about that, and, *mutatis mutandis,* if it might not be the case that the tub carefully disconnected itself from the wall, strolled out the bathroom on those little feet, down the hall past some of the bewildered but resigned faculty members, into the elevator (it is doubtful the tub could manage the steps), down to the ground floor, and out to freedom.

I could have lived with the absence of the tub. I might have rationalized its disappearance in any number of creative ways. But then, the wooden partitions, which formerly fit neatly around the tub, also dematerialized. A few days later there was a hole in the wall where the sink used to be.

After considerable thought on the matter, I decided I could not very well ignore all these signs -- God was trying to tell me something. In theological circles there is a strange but well accepted principle called *creatio ex nihilo,* where God, by virtue of his omnipotence, creates things out of nothing.

Here it seems God had whimsically turned the idea inside out. The Deity, probably with a wry grin on his cosmic face, was now in the process of "extinction out of something." He was, by holy fiat, beginning to will out of existence all the objects in the material universe. He was starting with the hardware in the fourth floor faculty bathroom. He would get around to the Empire State Building and Ronald Reagan sometime next month.

I have just returned from the rest room. The toilet is still there. So is the door. During my visit, I had what might be described as a Lutheran revelation. It is a discovery, I am afraid, that might invalidate my thesis. On the door, provided the door has not disappeared in the time it has taken to write this last paragraph down, is clearly and evenly penned the following message:

NOTICE
This rest room will be renovated
for office use. Work will start
9/20/83.
Thank you.

Now this new bit of information leaves me no less mystified. It's only mid-August and half of the bath room is already absent without leave. Also, I've done absolutely nothing in regard to this rest room for which I might honestly be thanked. I'm going to get to the bottom of this bathroom enigma.

That is, unless I mysteriously disapp

Baltimore Evening Sun, August, 1983.

*D*ie *Fliegen*

Graduate students in philosophy are always fun to watch. Perhaps more than any other discipline, philosophy attracts a strange collection of people. The small department here is loaded with them. They do not, as far as I can tell, awaken in the morning with the expressed intention of spending their day as exceedingly odd people, it just turns out that way.

One particular office in this department is shared by Alex, a 35 year old Scotsman who in his dress, but even more so in his demeanor and countenance, gives one the perpetual impression of having just been startled into consciousness five minutes earlier. For months, when I would visit his office-mate Andre, I falsely believed I had just awakened him from what Kant would call a "dogmatic slumber." Alex would sit there, at his desk, chin propped on his hands, unfocused eyes peering out through leadened lids and the thick lenses of oversized spectacles at what must seem to him an exceedingly fuzzy world.

Alex is doing his thesis on the "just war." Judging from his behavior around the office, he seems clearly to be anti-Augustinian, though one must admit any act of violence usually entails aggressive behavior which for Alex would appear to be a physical if not ethical impossibility.

My friend Andre, the office-mate, is German. In many ways he deserves to be the subject of his own study. For the present, however, it suffices to say that if there could be an embodiment of the German word *genau,* he would most surely be it. A few months back, one of the local people, an elderly woman, began to walk her dog in our courtyard. After examining for several days the tell-tale evidence of the dog's comings and goings, Andre placed a small, meticulously lettered plastic-covered sign on the bench at the *cul-de-sac:*

This is no dog's toilet.
The residents

Recently, in his office at the philosophy department, Andre has begun to take as a personal affront the fact that on chilly spring days *die Fliegen* (the flies) have begun to take refuge in the warm office which he and Alex share.

Consequently, Andre has began using Wittgenstein's *Philosophical Investigations* to dispatch *die Fliegen*. Earlier he had tried Russell's work in *Logical Atomism* but that opus proved to be unwieldy and, short of the remote possibility of being bored to death, the flies never seemed to succumb to the Englishman's work. Before his settling on Wittgenstein, I had suggested to Andre that he might try using Sartre's *Les Mouches,* but he informed me that since it was a literary work, and by an existentialist at that, it was too soft and would just not do for his purposes.

Alex was from the start, of course, diametrically opposed to the killing of *die Fliegen* on moral grounds. The myopic Scot would lecture his office-mate as the latter stalked around the room waiting for the unsuspecting *Fliegen* to rub their back legs together: "If you are not going to eat them, you should not kill them," intoned Alex. And so after Andre had methodically tracked the flies and subjected them to the full weight of all 600 propositions of the *Philosophical Investigations,* Alex would just as methodically line the flies up, one after the other on his desk, and with a gentle breath would vainly attempt to deliver a kind of *en masse* artificial resuscitation to this lifeless queue of still-winged creatures.

Needless to say, he was never very successful, though he once confided to me, but not to Andre, that if he could find some way of pinching their little noses while he blew, he might have a much higher survival rate.

Die Fliegen are not the only topic of dispute between these young philosophers. Other somewhat acrimonious but nonviolent shirmishes periodically break out between them. Andre, for example, is a heavy smoker and when Alex's mother heard of this serious breach with personal as well as communal decorum she immediately had delivered to their office an air-purifier, accompanied by a loving note instructing her son "to keep the Hun under control."

But the one item which seems to bother Andre the most about Alex is that the latter may well be the cheapest man in all of Britain. Each day on the way to the office, for example, Alex makes a stop at Boots, the local drug store, to grab a dab of cologne from the sample counter in the men's toiletries section. Andre swears Alex takes two squirts on Saturday to tide him over for the weekend.

For several months before Alex received his educational grant, he would consume plain boiled water at tea time, apparently unable to afford the extravagance of tea bags or instant coffee. Now that he is in the money, he has purchased some generic brand tea bags, each pouch receiving a thorough workout before it is laid to rest next to the flies in his waste paper basket.

The other day I went around to see Andre before a seminar we are attending together. As we sat in the office chatting and watching Alex use a particular tea bag for the sixth time, we heard a piercing scream come from the office next door. More particularly, the scream had emanated from Ian, a short stubble-faced graduate student from Oxford, who always screams whenever he has an important philosophical thought. Alex doesn't like Ian screaming. He sometimes wishes out loud that Ian didn't have so many good ideas, or maybe that he might transfer to another department. I don't know how to tell Alex, there is no other department for Ian.

Unpublished, April, 1984.

Philosophers' Mall

Professor S.J. Sisyphus had just finished frantically searching through the last of his desk drawers. He sat back uneasily in his swivel chair and stared above his desk at the picture of Demosthenes talking about philosophy with marbles in his mouth. There was really no getting around it. A new semester was about to begin and the professor had completely run out of philosophical insights. He had looked throughout his office. He searched at home as well. He even sneaked a peak at a colleague's desk top, vainly hoping a stray philosophical thought or two might have been left behind on the blotter. The results were all the same: Sisyphus was tapped out of trenchant philosophical reflections, just as his classes were returning from the Christmas holiday.

In academic circles, a man is known by his ideas, or, barring those, his appropriation and embroidering of others' thoughts. Sisyphus seemed to be fresh out in both departments. He checked the campus book store. He looked throughout the library. When he inquired whether they would be expecting any new insights soon, the reference librarian shrugged her shoulders and whispered, "There's really no way of telling. You know how these things are."

The professor wandered back to his office. The walk in the clear, crisp air allowed him to come to terms with his alternatives. He realized he had but one chance left. He would have to travel to Philsophers' Mall.

When Sisyphus arrived at the mall, it was with a great deal of apprehension. It all looked so big and impressive. There were after Christmas sales everywhere. He didn't know quite where to begin. He walked to the center of the mall. There he found the fountain and accompanying pool -- ornate structures, classical in design, with jets of water spouting from the mouths of life-sized figures representing Aristotle and the peripetetics.

Across from the fountain he found the mall directory, a large, flat illuminated structure of multi-colored plastic and wood. On its plexi-glass surface could be seen a detailed map of the mall. "This has obviously been the work of a nihilist," the professor mumbled to himself. The directory included a large red movable arrow on which was printed in clear black letters: "You are not here."

Sisyphus had a sudden feeling of vertigo. It was not clear whether its source was the dizzying affect of the directory, or the overcooked Spinoza-burger and fries he had hastily consumed at the fast food stand just inside the mall entrance. He wandered aimlessly past the action posters of Kierkegaard and Kant displayed in the windows of the Idea Outlet. He hurried by the childrens' store, Plato-n-Things, and past the impressive blue and white sign welcoming the solipcists' convention to the mall. Finally, he found himself standing at the display window of the House of Insights.

The place was crawling with graduate students bickering over who had legitimate claim to various major and minor premises strewn atop a sales counter. A small bespectacled man refused to relinquish a conclusion he held tightly in his fist, as a much larger man, a phenomenologist, held just a tightly to the two premises that led to the conclusion. They tugged back and forth on the argument until it lost its valid form.

Professor Sisyphus picked through a bin marked, "Realizations, new and used, 50% off." He found a dog-eared *cogito ergo sum* and a badly soiled *esse est percipi* or two, but there was nothing fresh to be found there. For a while, he stared vacantly at a display case full of conundrums and paradoxes. A few mathematicians crowded him away from the case, but there was really nothing there the panicky philosopher could use.

Sisyphus left the House of Insights a nearly broken man. As he walked to the end of the mall, he watched a man in a blue work shirt, with the name "Ludwig" stitched above the left breast pocket, push a broom full of discarded theses and antitheses tossed away by a gang of young Hegelians who seem to do little more than hang around the mall.

By now, Sisyphus had been from one end of the mall to the other. There were only a few stores remaining. The hour was late and the philosopher was tired and depressed. He walked past the Thought Explosion. He stopped in front of Syllogisms-n-Stuff to collect his thoughts. Gaudy Venn-diagrams equipped with small left-over Christmas lights blinked on and off. The professor gazed beyond the promenade to the Lyceum, the large department store. It was all that stood between Sisyphus and the parking lot.

When he entered the Lyceum's elevator on the ground floor, a small voice within him whispered to push the button for the third floor. When the grey doors of the elevator parted, the scales from his eyes were at the same time lifted. It was as if he had been moved by some great but unknowable Mall Manager. His search for ideas had come to an end. Professor Sisyphus found himself in the midst of the department of notions.

🍎   Unpublished, December, 1986.

THE BOMB

*There will one day spring forth from the brain of science
a machine or force so fearful in its potentialities,
so absolutely terrifying that even man the fighter,
who will dare torture and death
in order to inflict torture and death,
will be appalled.*

-- Thomas Edison

The Dragon and the Turtle

Once upon a time there were four brothers who each had been blessed by the gods with a special gift. The first had the amazing capacity to reconstruct an entire skeleton from the smallest fragment of bone. The second had learned to give flesh and muscle to the bare frame of any creature. The third brother had mastered the art of adding hair and teeth to the naked skin of any beast. But the most uncanny gift of all was possessed by the fourth brother -- he was blessed with a knack for breathing life into the carcass of any lifeless creature.

One day the four brothers entered the woods in search of a sliver of bone, so that each of them might demonstrate his particular skill. After hours of searching, they came upon a very small but unmistakable piece of bone. But because it seemed part of an extinct creature, they did not know the nature of the beast whose fragment they had found.

The first brother, though not entirely sure of what he was doing, reconstructed a skeleton from the small piece. The second was no less confused, but managed to give muscle and flesh to the new frame. Hair and teeth were carefully added by the third. And the fourth brother warily breathed life in the creature's huge nostrils. A moment later, the fruit of the brothers' collective labor, a huge dragon, stood before them. And with one movement of its giant tongue, the monster swallowed the four brothers in one gigantic bite.

These early days of August mark the anniversary of the dropping of the atomic bombs on Hiroshima and Nagasaki. Each of the weapons' creators, at the University of Chicago, at the White House, in Los Alamos, and in the air above these Japanese cities, added his special skill to the construction and deployment of another strange and terrifying beast whose fury was unleashed in the shattered nuclei of atoms.

Each year at this time some of these participants are interviewed. We listen to them and nod our heads. But most of the debate and discussion that arises each August seems to center on the ethical implications of the circumstances surrounding the bombing of these particular cities in early August of 1945.

Would we have suffered one million American casualties had we not chosen to drop the bomb? Did President Truman have other viable and less cataclysmic alternatives? Were the Nazis close to the completion of their own atomic weapon? The answers to these questions are important. Since the war, they have loomed large in the minds of countless redactive historians of all persuasions. But the quest for answers to these questions somehow becomes dwarfed by a larger unnamed query which rests uneasily in the backs of all our minds: Does the fate of the four brothers await us all?

I was not alive to hear of the bombing first hand. I was part of the post-war baby boom. I have, however, grown up with it. We grew together, beast and boy, beast and man, both becoming more sophisticated, both able to accomplish a great deal more than before.

My parents were born in a Newtonian world. I arrived in a world where $E = mc^2$, a world where the future is merely an option. Both generations now carry the unnamed possibility around with them. It resides in the backs of our heads. It hangs there like a 15-watt bulb in a dark and musty corner of the basement. We rarely, if ever, go there, but the bulb is never turned off.

It was switched on for my parents' generation in August 1945. For myself and my siblings, it became illuminated early on, during incomprehensible air raid drills where we hid under our wood and wrought-iron desks and prayed the sound we heard was merely the 1 p.m. Monday whistle commemorating the dead of another war. Now a better informed and more pragmatic generation of school children no longer seeks refuge from the beast by huddling under their desks.

The natural world was destroyed that day in August of 1945. It was at once reconstituted by a perverse form of magic, complete with a new vision. It has taken us many years to get clear on just what the proper content of that vision may be. By now, however, it is certain that it no longer involves sitting in underground civil defense stations until the coast is clear. On August 6 of every year, we rummage to the back of the basement to find the real image. It is still there. It is made no less horrible by our lack of attention.

There is a perhaps apocryphal story that used to circulate in academic circles about one of the great atomic physicists who, like the four brothers, lent his particular talents to the construction of an awesome beast. Since the unleashing of that beast, the little bulb in the back of his skull has burned brighter than most.

Years later, the scientist was wandering in the woods with a companion, when he came upon a small land turtle. Thinking that his children would be pleased with the tortoise, the physicist placed it in his pocket and started home. After a few steps, however, he paused, and then carefully retrieved the turtle from his coat pocket.

Then the scientist retraced his steps, and thoughtfully returned the tortoise to precisely the spot where it had been discovered, leaving it to wander where it might. When the friend inquired as to what the physicist was doing, he looked pensively at his companion and answered: "It just occurred to me that for one man, I've already tampered enough with nature." Each year on August 6 we are reminded of that tampering.

                                         Baltimore Evening Sun, August, 1983.

No Man Will Venture Farther

Sometime early in Christmas week of 1768, the British astronomer and explorer, Captain James Cook, began his first frigid and treacherous voyage to the southernmost regions of the Pacific, and beyond to search for a *terra incognita,* the undiscovered continent of Antarctica. It was as haunting a tale as Odysseus' passage through a bewitched Mediterranean full of lotus-eaters, blinded cyclopses, and tempting sirens. Cook's orders were to find the unknown land at the bottom of the world -- a world as yet too vast to have been accurately charted.

In his first voyage, Cook did not find the elusive frozen continent. In a second attempt, in 1774, he unwittingly came within 70 miles of it -- seeing the looming, blue-white beauty of the ice-alps from a distance -- before turning back. The ice jams had become so packed, his ship could no longer maneuver. Through a pervasive grey mist, he had mistaken the jagged cliffs of Antarctica for a collection of inconsequential icebergs. Cook, after all, was made of the same stuff as Odysseus. As the ancient wanderer informs us, "I am a man, not a god." Still, even in Cook's defeat, he was able to write confidently in 1774, "If I can be so bold to say no man will venture farther than I have done."

Exactly 200 years later, on December 24, 1968, Frank Borman, James Lovell and William Anders completed two rotations of the earth and then headed for their ultimate destintion -- ten revolutions above the dusty and pock-marked surface of the moon. They had traveled 231,000 miles from Cape Kennedy, their port of departure. While in orbit, the reflection of the entire earth's surface could be seen on the tempered glass of the tiniest window of their space craft. When the *Apollo 8* astronauts splashed down on December 27, it was to a much smaller Pacific than the one in which James Cook wandered for the better part of six years, searching for something he died thinking did not exist.

Cook spent the peace of Christmas 1768 in silent foreboding waters -- seas populated by strange ice formations and troubled grey albatrosses gliding overhead in utter silence. The American astronauts began their return voyage to earth on December 25. When they fired their *Saturn V* rockets which took them out of their orbit 70 miles above the surface of the moon, the boosters made no sound. It was as lonely a place as men had ever been. Like the journey of Odysseus there was enough portention in the voyage of Cook and that of the astronauts to desire the peace and safety of home.

But peace on earth has come to mean something quite different in the two centuries since Cook's travels. Earlier in his career, during the Seven Years' War, Cook had proven himself in combat on the turbulent seas of two of the world's vast oceans. The war had involved every major European power of his day. But upon its bloody completion in 1763, the Seven Years' War had changed the face of Europe very little.

While *Apollo 8* made its way to the moon, 82 crewman of the American ship, *The Pueblo*, were released by North Korea after the United States signed a document admitting the ship had been in North Korean waters. Unlike the Seven Years' War, the "*Pueblo* incident" was not a conflict which involved all the major powers of the world, but, with one small mistake, it might have been the impetus for dramatically and tragically changing the contours of the entire planet.

Since the flight of *Apollo 8,* the world has become an even smaller place. The vast space through which Borman and his crew traveled can now more clearly be seen, at least in cosmic terms, as in the neighborhood. During the 250 years between Magellan and Cook, the period of the great explorations, the size of the known world increased tenfold. From 1917 to 1932, the beginning of modern physics, the dimensions of the known universe increased 1 trillion times.

If the size of our entire solar system could fit in the chipped coffee cup resting on the edge of my desk, our galaxy would be larger than Cook's elusive Antarctica. It has been estimated by contemporary physicists that there have been 100 billion galaxies, each of them containing billions of stars greater and lesser than our sun. We are, collectively, a tiny speck in a constantly expanding and near-infinite universe. We aren't Russians and Americans, we are residents of the same infinitesimally small place.

Yet, this week on earth we prepare for the peace of Christmas while talking of arming the small parcel of space around our tiny planet with satellites equipped with death rays. And I wonder, in the late evening, when all the shoppers have gone to bed, if there will be a Christmas in 2168. I wonder if on some distant planet in the not too distant future they might not say of us, "No one ventured farther than they." I wonder if they may not quote Odysseus: "They were men, not gods."

Baltimore Evening Sun, December, 1985.

*H*iroshima: *Nightmare of War to Nightmare of Peace*

I am become Death, the shaker of worlds.
--Robert Oppenheimer

Having invented a new Holocaust And been the first with it to win a war, How they make haste to cry with fingers crossed, King's X -- no fair to use it anymore.
--Robert Frost

On August 6, 1945, at 8:16 a.m., the *Enola Gay,* an American B-29 bomber named after the mother of its pilot, Colonel Paul Tibbets, dropped a fire extinguisher-shaped cannister over the Japanese city of Hiroshima. The silver cylinder contained a uranium bomb, nicknamed "Little Boy." After a 28,000-foot descent by parachute, a timing device tripped its trigger mechanism. A fraction of a second later -- a portion of time too small for any 1940's watch to measure -- a tiny dot of amethyst-colored light expanded to a glowing, purplish-red fireball. At the center of this thousand-foot glowing mass, the temperature had reached 50 million degrees.

On the ground, directly below the explosion, the temperature leveled out at several thousand degrees centigrade. Half of the city's mixed military and civilian population was affected instantly; 70,000 were killed at once, another 70,000 were critically injured. Some 62,000 of the 90,000 buildings standing before 8:16 that morning were destroyed instantly. Of the city's 200 physicians, 180 were killed or incapacitated by 8:30 a.m. Only three of Hiroshima's 55 hospitals and first aid stations remained intact.

On that 1945 day at 8:16 a.m., the world had been abruptly notified of the coming of the Atomic Age. Human beings now had at their disposal a force capable of leveling entire cities, or perhaps, destroying the entire planet.

In the past 40 years that realization has brought with it an understanding that we, like Mary Shelly's Dr. Frankenstein, have become unwitting victims of our own invention. It is as if we had awakened from a nightmare of war, only to find a nightmare of peace.

The genesis of this waking nightmare is sometimes obscured by a curious kind of national mythology that has arisen around the dropping of the bomb. It is a peculiar brand of myth-making, not only because the elements that constitute it are strongly held beliefs, but also because many of these beliefs are simply not true.

At the time of the dropping of the bomb on Japan, most Americans rejoiced over the ending of the war. The bomb was believed to be a legitimate combat weapon that had brought a more expeditious victory, while saving American lives which surely would have been lost in a land invasion of Japan.

It was also generally believed that other alternatives to dropping the bombs on Hiroshima and Nagasaki, such as demonstrating the bomb in an uninhabited area or warning Japanese civilians before the blasts, were thoroughly discussed and debated before they were rejected in the summer of 1945.

Upon closer analysis of the historical record, however, a good case can be made that both beliefs are untrue. Although they continue to serve as the foundations of our most widespread national convictions about the moral appropriateness of the dropping of the bomb, both beliefs are based on meager evidence.

By August of 1945, American forces were securely based on Iwo Jima, Okinawa, and other strategic islands in the Pacific. For months our fleet had been cruising unmolested off the

Japanese coast. American submarines regularly patrolled large stretches of water in the Sea of Japan. Because of these and other developments, Hanson Baldwin, a military affairs analyst, has pointed out, "Food was short, mines, submarines, surface vessels and planes clamped an iron blockade around the main islands; raw materials were scarce. Blockade, bombing and unsuccessful attempts at dispersion had reduced Japanese production capacity by 20 to 60 percent." Germany had been defeated. Japan now faced the prospect of fighting a war on two fronts, for Russia had entered the Pacific war on August 8. That was the day before the United States was to drop a second bomb, the plutonium "Fat Man", on the city of Nagasaki.

It is clear the dropping of the bombs on Hiroshima and Nagasaki hastened the end of the war. It is not clear, however, that it was the only way to bring the Pacific conflict to a close. The War Department's estimate -- that 500,000 to 1 million men would be killed in a land invasion of Japan -- was made in April of 1945. The invasion of the southern islands by the Allied forces was to occur in November, with a mainland invasion to follow in 1946, if necessary. The atomic bombs were dropped a full seven months before the scheduled mainland invasion. With the Soviet Union entered in the war, drastically reduced war production in Japan, and a consolidated Allied effort in the Pacific, it is highly unlikely that the War Department's grim prediction would have been shown correct.

The truth of the other belief about the dropping of the bomb -- that we explored other options before its deployment -- is equally suspect. Some evidence suggests that as early as April of 1945 the British were led to believe the United States fully intended to use the bomb for military purposes.

On April 30, Sir H.M. Wilson, head of the British Joint Staff Mission in Washington, had informed his government, "The

Americans propose to drop a bomb in August." Wilson went on to raise two connected questions: "Do we agree the weapons should be used against the Japanese? If for any reason we did not, the matter would presumably have to be raised by the Prime Minister with the President. If we do agree, various points still arise on which it would be desirable to have consultations with the Americans...whether any warning should be given to the Japanese." These discussions between Churchill and Truman were never to take place.

A week earlier, on April 25, Henry Stimson, the Secretary of War, met with the new president, Harry Truman, to discuss the deployment of the bomb. At that meeting, Stimson received Truman's approval to establish an Interim Committee "for recommending action to the executive and legislative branches of our government when secrecy is no longer in full effect (and also) actions to be taken by the War Department prior to that time in the anticipation of the post-war problems." One of the more profound ironies in this tale is the virtual absence of participation by the legislative branch from that day until the mushroom-shaped cloud formed over Hiroshima.

By June 11, the committee, which consisted of Stimson, two college presidents, the head of an insurance company, the undersecretary of the navy, and James Byrnes, a special assistant to the president, had recommended: (1) The bomb should be used against Japan as soon as possible. (2) It should be used on a dual target -- that is, a military installation or war plant surrounding or adjacent to houses and other buildings more susceptible to damage. And (3) it should be used without warning.

The Interim Committee had been helped in its two-day deliberation by a Special Scientific Advisory Panel made up of four eminent physicists: Enrico Fermi, Ernest Lawrence, Arthur Compton and Robert Oppenheimer. All but Oppenheimer were

Nobel Prize recipients. All had been involved in some stage of the planning, design and development of the bomb. None had any formal training in ethics or policy making. June 1 was the only day the full Interim Committee together was to consider other alternatives to the dropping of the bomb on mixed civilian and military populations.

The sources for reconstructing the debate consist of Arthur Compton's book, *Atomic Quest;* James Byrnes' memoirs, *All in One Lifetime;* the exchange of letters between Ernest Lawrence and a friend in August of 1945; and the diaries of Henry Stimson.

All agree the idea of a demonstration was mentioned in passing at the morning session. Shortly after 1 p.m. the group adjourned for lunch. The men sat at four small tables making the general sharing of ideas rather difficult. According to Compton's account, the discussion of alternatives began when Stimson asked him whether some sort of demonstration might bring about the end of the war.

By Byrnes' account, it was he who engaged Lawrence in conversation about a demonstration. By whatever means the discussion began, however, all accounts agree it was Oppenheimer who was skeptical, doubting if any sufficiently startling demonstration could be devised to convince the Japanese to surrender. At one point in the exchange, Byrnes mentioned a fear the Japanese might bring American prisoners to a demonstration site. Several other participants inquired about the repercussions of a failed demonstration.

In retrospect, another one of the more profound ironies of this story is that the epicenter of the device exploded over Hiroshima was directly above the ancient castle that served as the location of an American prisoners of war camp. It was completely destroyed by the bomb. The mortality rate of its occupants, who included prisoners, soldiers, and school girls who acted as ticket takers for the museum, is estimated at over 90 percent. This becomes all the more ironic when considering Lawrence's account of the June 1 discussion. Lawrence suggests the entire discussion of alternatives lasted no longer than ten minutes and it was Oppenheimer and Byrnes who put a damper on the brief possibility that there might have been a demonstration detonation or a warning before hand.

On at least three occasions in September and December of 1944, and in March of 1945, attempts were made to get Stimson to seriously consider the possibility of a demonstration or a warning. The last of these was made by General Marshall, the Army Chief of Staff, just a few days before the June 1 meeting. General Marshall had emphasized to Stimson the importance of at least giving the Japanese notice: "Every effort should be made to keep our record of warning clear."

In light of the fact the British seemed to know in early spring of 1945 of our intentions to drop the bomb in August, it is not unreasonable to suggest that the June 1 discussion was a cursory one because Truman and Stimson had long since made up their minds that as soon as the bomb was ready, we would use it on a civilian-military target. Byrnes may well have been sent to the June 1 meeting with instructions from Truman to steer opinion in that direction.

If this analysis is correct, it may tell us something important, not just about our deeply held belief that the end justifies the means, but also that the end may be effected by any means. If we accept this moral dictum, as Truman and Stimson appear to have done, we remain oblivious to the ethical realization that was to be made in the aftermath of August 6, 1945:

Give order that these bodies
High on a stage be placed to the view;
And let me speak to the yet unknowing world
How these things came about; so shall you hear
Of carnal, bloody and unnatural acts,
Of accidental judgments, casual slaughters,
Of deaths put on by cunning and forced cause,
And, in the upshot, purposes mistook
Fallen on inventor's heads...
Even while men's minds are wild, lest more mischance
On plots and errors happen.
--Hamlet

Baltimore Evening Sun, August, 1985.

The Dancing Class
of Nuclear Initiatives

Recently a colleague of mine, a bright, refined and attractively self-effacing Dominican nun, relayed to me a story from her school days in Scotland. It seems she had finished high school a year early and, since it was the practice to begin university at the age of 18, her father thought it advisable that she spend the year leading to that magic age of majority living in England and attending finishing school. It is there my friend learned the intricacies of a number of important domestic arts, as well as a variety of steps that go into the making of waltzes, foxtrots, boxsteps, and a tango or two.

The instructor in these ballroom dips, glides and twirls was a Miss White, a small woman with an exceedingly craggy face, perhaps the result of years of teaching what today would be called the dancing impaired. She also possessed great, disjuncted shocks of white hair which stood straight up on end by some minor electrical miracle. These two contradictory qualities gave her appearance the net effect of looking as though her hair had been permanently frightened years before by some heinous event about which her face had not yet received the news.

But the most remarkable aspect to Miss White's instruction was that she apparently did it all by remote control. She would sit properly upright in a wooden folding chair, in much the same fashion as her hair arranged itself on the top of her head, and instruct students in the finer points of a rumba without so much as moving a muscle, save those connected to her surely wrinkled larynx.

The young women of her classes mysteriously managed to learn these rather intricate dances through some kind of telekinesis or perhaps a long distance strain of parapsychological osmosis, unknown, I should think, to the world's foremost psychics or cellular biologists.

Because her studio seemed to be pervaded with a perpetual chill, Miss White, the unmoved mover, took to wearing two snow white muffs around her hands and feet.

There were constant arguments, however, as to whether they really were muffs. Some of the more discerning students had suggested that they might in fact be twin, deeply comatose Shitzus or Malteses, two very breeds of small dogs resembling a certain kind of fuzzy and discarded, but nonetheless, immaculate bedroom slippers.

Indeed, it may very well have been that the muffs were small dogs who, through the aid of many years of obedience school, were now practicing the same Zen-like discipline of motionlessness as their master. At any rate, the identity of the muffs remains an enigma to be fussed over by the kinds of people who worry about whether life imitates art or if the reverse may be closer to the truth.

Despite its miraculous nature, there was still one major problem with Miss White's instruction. There were no men to be found at the finishing school. Consequently, the larger girls were taught the gentleman's lead, while the more petite young ladies were instructed to follow.

Now it also came to pass that Miss White took her uncanny skills to the boy's military academy across the road, where she, for want of suitable female partners, taught the smaller cadets the part of the young ladies, while the larger boys worked earnestly at osmotically committing the intricate and elaborate steps of the gentlemen to memory.

In the spring, she brought the two schools together. The result was, of course, inevitable.

I tell this story now for I fear it may be a metaphor for American foreign policy. For those of you who have been watching our latest nuclear initiatives, I need give no further exposition.

As the Talmud suggests, the rest would be merely commentary.

Baltimore Evening Sun, March, 1984.

*O*n a Tiny, Fragile Planet

Snow falls and sleep is difficult. Outside, behind a veil of clouds, the stars are wide awake. In the summer months, they always seem more easily detectable, much closer than they do now. This evening, they are mute and shrouded -- invisible night travelers on a silent journey of such immense proportion that by my next sleepless encounter with them they will have moved near-infinite distances.

Inside, on the night table by the bed, ticks a small oddly-shaped alarm clock. It only seems to work when laid on its Victorian face. Throughout the darkness it counts an anonymous time until finally a tiny bell within it will signal the end of night.

In the next room, a darkened kitchen, small, perfectly shaped droplets of water fall slowly from the spigot to a waiting coffee cup below. This dripping cadence seems detectable only in these late night hours.

I sit in a rocking chair by the window. My only light is supplied by an eerie luminous effect given off by the untouched snow. Because of the white blanket's brightness, the color of night is transformed into a dark, vibrant blue. As I rock back and forth, the arcs of wood on the bottom of the chair make a rhythmic creaking sound, like that of a worn metronome. If I am perfectly still, within the mortal cage of my ribs I can feel another metronome beating. It too keeps an anonymous time until finally a small alarm within it will signal the end of night. In the summer, on these sleepless nights, the ticking field crickets count with me. In the dead of winter, it is done alone.

As a child, I was terrified of the dark: a charter member of that large fraternal order of children whose solidarity lies solely in the belief in the proposition that far more lies in wait under the bed than puffy grey dust balls our mothers might have missed. In childhood, I often spent these fitful, sleepless nights conjuring up unspeakable demons who crouched ominously in secret domestic places that in daylight were only inhabited by old shoes, worn straight brooms and stacks of old magazines. Years later, I have found one doesn't so much need to use his imagination in the fashioning of demons.

As an adult, I have learned there are those things in life just as frightening, but a great deal more real, than the childhood phantoms. Now, if the monsters return at night, it is usually because I have seen them on the news and have later summoned them in a dream. Sleep has become that time when all the unsorted stuff comes flying out, as from a large metal trash can upset in high wind. It is for this reason I now rise from bed and go to the rocker. There are those things in life that will not go away simply by rolling over on the other ear.

This evening I have been rocking back and forth while thinking about pictures of the earth as seen from space. In these photographs, like nowhere else, we can clearly discern that humankind lives on the face of a tiny, mist-enshrouded ball drifting through unfathomable darkness.

Tonight, I have been thinking about the new proposed budget of the United State government. It calls for an expenditure of $285 billion for defense. Included in that amount is $9.7 billion which is to go into the research, development and deployment of nuclear weapons.

Admittedly, it is very difficult to comprehend the meaning of the concept "billion", particularly in the dead of night. But I have little trouble understanding that the combined total of $29 billion suggested for education, jobs and social services seems dwarfed when standing alongside that $285 billion.

Much earlier tonight, on the evening news, I was told the president believes that $285 billion will make our tiny, mist-enshrouded planet a much safer place on which to live. I listened very attentively to that suggestion. And now, I am sitting up in the middle of the night rocking back and forth.

A few moments ago, I suddenly remembered the face of a little man I saw only once several years ago. He was slightly overweight, balding, with a round face and large dark eyes. His job was to sit in a tiny bunker, deep beneath the Catoctin mountains, not far from Camp David. Every day he would sit (and for all I know still sits) and wait by a small desk that faces a white wall on which is placed a round, perfectly synchronized clock. He was there diligently to record the precise starting time in the event of a nuclear confrontation. By now, I should think, he had been replaced by an electronic device of some sort, perhaps to be paid for by part of that $285 billion.

And so, as I rock back and forth, I can hear coming from my kitchen the sound of perfectly formed droplets of water hitting a waiting coffee cup. I can feel the fist-sized muscle within my chest contracting and relaxing. Across the room, on the table by the bed, I can hear the Victorian clock ticking face down. And this evening, in the middle of the night, I could almost swear I hear the sound of a perfectly synchronized clock buried deep within the Catoctin mountains, beating its anonymous time.

Baltimore Evening Sun, February, 1985.

Nothing

> Nothing is but what is not.
> *--Macbeth*

Holes. There is something about them that fascinates -- particularly if they are found in the ground. I began thinking about all this when an earnest looking man on a large yellow backhoe began creating an immense hole in the grass and asphalt behind the building in which I teach. After two days work, man and machine had fashioned a fair-size crater. For the next few days, the backhoe operator and several co-workers gathered around and intently gazed into the hole. Periodically, a passer-by or two would stop to join in the reverie.

I must admit, at the time, to thinking all this rather silly -- several grown people standing around staring into a yawning hole in the ground -- until it occured to me what the real object of their attention was. It was not the hole itself. It was what the hole contained: nothing.

Early one morning, just to make sure I was not misinterpreting the amazed looks on their faces, I approached a gaggle of the construction workers standing at the edge of the precipice. Most of them stood with chapped hands stuffed in the pockets of work trousers, their squinting eyes focused on the bottom of the pit. I asked one very bluntly: "Excuse me, could you tell me what the big fascination is with this hole?" "Nothing," he replied knowingly. "Absolutely nothing. Can't you see we are busy here?"

I returned to my office where I pulled the *Encyclopedia of Philosophy* from the shelf. There, in volume six, nestled between "Norwegian Philosophy" and the 18th century German romantic, Novalis, was "Nothing" -- complete with bibliography. Noted for his important contributions to nothing, P.L. Heath, a contemporary British philosopher, spends 1,159 words in a succinct and compelling essay on the contours of nothing. He begins the article with some valuable information:

> "Nothing is an awe-inspiring yet essentially undigested concept highly esteemed by writers of a mystical nature but by most others regarded with anxiety, nausea and panic. Nobody seems to know how to deal with it, though plain persons generally are reported to have little difficulty in saying, seeing, hearing or doing nothing."

I sat back in my desk chair and let nothing sink in. In an instant several things began to fall into place, like the tumblers of a locked chest containing a great mystery. Before that moment, I could never understand anything the German philosopher, Martin Heidegger, had ever written. He uses very difficult German, often inventing his own words *ex nihilo*. All this goes into the making of very difficult books full of sentences like: "Man is in awe at the possibility of a hole in being."

But now it was crystal clear to me: several construction workers were gathered behind Gibbons Hall awed at the possibility of a hole in being. It all made great sense.

This explanation also goes a long way in solving the vexing question about why there are so many pot-holes in our city streets. Earnest, hard-working crews, equipped with smoking pots of asphalt, are dispatched each morning to the pot-hole scenes. But when they arrive, they get a good look at these pits and are immediately awed by the possibility of holes in being. This, of course, is precisely why these workers always seem to be leaning on their shovels, their faces dazed by a close brush with nothing.

Of course, it stands to reason the larger the hole in being, the greater quantity of nothing one may encounter. A hole is always a hole in something. The larger the something, the greater the possibility of nothing, the clearer the possibility of being awed. If you doubt this, consider for a moment the Grand Canyon. Several thousand tourists a summer drive day and night so they may pitch a tent by the side of the road and walk to the edge of nothing just to have a good look.

There is also perhaps a political and moral tale to be told in all this worrying about nothing. This realization of the awe-inspiring character of nothing, coupled with the notion that the greater the something, the larger the possibility of nothing, may help us better to understand the recent lack of genuine progress at the Geneva summit talks, as well as this weeks' sword-rattling in the direction of Libya.

What better way to guarantee the possibility of the large scale existence of nothing than failure to make any real progress on discussions of arms control, or to talk of invading a country, ruled by a tyrannical madman, but which sits in the middle of the world like so much kindling waiting for a match. In one of Bertolt Brecht's plays he asks a very important question: "What happens to the hole when the cheese is gone?"

Baltimore Evening Sun, January, 1986.

Moral Forgetting

> Memory is not just the imprint of the past upon us; it is the keeper of what is meaningful for our deepest hopes and fears.
> --Rollo May

Deep in the hearts and minds of all but the barely sentient of us there seems to exist an omnipresent tension -- a small but important battle waged in the recesses of our grey matter. It is a struggle between the longing to remember and a tendency, or perhaps a need, to forget. Each of us experiences the tension of these opposing forces in our own way. There are those who are blessed, or perhaps sometimes cursed, with uncanny recall. Others find it difficult to remember even the most important and poignant of moments. Between those two extremes most of the rest of us live our lives.

Although psychologists before and after Freud have argued the issue, it is difficult to decide with any certainty whether there really is such a thing as unintentional forgetting. It is safe to say, however, that one of the best measures of an individual, or an entire culture for that matter, is what he or it remembers, as well as what remains buried and forgotten.

Loren Eiseley, the poet and anthropologist, in one of his beautiful essays discusses a bizarre case in which he was called in to help identify a suicide victim who had so carefully effaced all his individuating characteristics that it was impossible to say who the man had been. The *rigor mortal* stranger was a real example of what had been created by Martin Smith in *Gorky Park* with one important difference: it was Eiseley's anonymous dead man who was responsible for his own effacement and oblivion.

One element that continually fascinates me about the reading of history is that sometimes in the story of mankind we can see that entire cultures, or at least large portions of them, have attempted the practice of Eiseley's dead stranger. The tombs and monuments of Iknaten, the father of solar monotheism, were defaced and rendered anonymous shortly after his death. The entire ancient city of Carthage appears to have been similarly erased by the Romans. The makers of the French revolution in the late 18th century attempted to destroy the Christian calendar and thus, they hoped, eliminate the last vestiges of bourgeois Christian morality. In our own time, each succeeding edition of the *Soviet Encyclopedia* graphically illustrates the point

The beginning of the Second World War, however, saw an important and regrettable moral change. It began in September of 1939 when Hitler ordered the bombing of Warsaw, where large numbers of civilians were destroyed. In January of 1940, Winston Churchill characterized obliteration bombing as "a new and odious form of attack." A few months earlier, before the United States became involved in the war, President Roosevelt sent a message to the German and Polish governments denouncing "the ruthless bombing from the air of civilians in unfortified centers of population." In that letter written at the end of 1939, Roosevelt suggested the bombings of Warsaw and Rotterdam "profoundly shocked the conscience of humanity." He concluded his plea this way: "I am therefore addressing this urgent appeal to every government to affirm its determination that its armed forces shall in no event and under no circumstances undertake bombardment from the air of civilian populations or unfortified cities."

By May of 1940, five months after Churchill's excoriation of obliteration bombing, Germany had captured Poland, Denmark, Norway, and was threatening to overrun Belgium, Holland and Luxembourg. Britain began the large scale bombing of German cities. Germany, in August of that same year, retaliated with attacks on airfields and fighter planes in southern England. From August of 1940 to June of 1941 thousands of German planes pounded at British ports and industrial centers. More than 40,000 British civilians were killed. Churchill announced that Germany was to be subjected to "an ordeal, the like of which has never been experienced by any country." A year later, in 1942 he asserted, "There are no sacrifices we will not make, no lengths of violence to which we will not go." By then, the cycle of moral forgetting had been set in motion. It continued as Hamburg, Berlin, Dresden, Pearl Harbor, London, Hiroshima, and Nagasaki were leveled.

Today, of course, it is difficult to find a civilized industrial nation that does not take the wholesale killing of civilians as a commonplace element of modern warfare. An entire generation of Americans and Russians have grown to adulthood with that common shared conviction. Indeed, it is the principle on which modern atomic arsenals were built and continue to grow.

In the process, an entire race of people seems to have forgotten the moral vision which gave rise to that editorial written in London in 1914. All over the world, we now accept as a grim matter of course a moral deficiency that has taken that moral vision's place. On this day, forty one years after the dropping of the bomb on Hiroshima, it is time for some moral remembering.

Baltimore Evening Sun, August, 1986.

VAGRANT THOUGHTS

Life is the art of drawing sufficient conclusions from insufficient premises.

🍎 -- *Samuel Butler*

Gifts of the Fall

Each morning I am awakened by the birds. In the summer months, robins and sparrows congregate in the yard like disgruntled street people waiting for breakfast. They are loud and impatient. They often butt in line, but their greed can be excused: though the noise makes it clear they are fond of the sound of their own voices, they are guilty of little more than loving too much the company of their own kind. These summer birds seem to live in the moment, or perhaps more clearly put, in a succession of eternally present moments.

A few weeks after the beginning of a new school year, things begin to change. Every year it becomes a little easier to comprehend that fall is rapidly approaching: the voices at morning-call begin to dwindle from a raucous din to a few plaintive songs. What on early August mornings had sounded like the voices of a hundred small children chattering in as many languages gradually subsides to a chilly silence punctuated by the sound of a single blackbird. The lonely bird does not sing a song; perhaps he is thinking out loud. Sparse, naked syllables stand between silence and silence. Robins are nowhere to be found. I must make myself arise for school; the more sociable birds are no longer here to assist me.

Just before dawn, a few crows fly overhead. They are not like the summer birds. They are aloof and solitary. In autumn, crows move above like disturbed black memories. The birds rise and fall but never seem to come to rest.

The sun has risen to fill the silence with a new light, but it is a fading light. A single luminous shaft of light that a few weeks ago stretched across the floor to my bed now falls several feet short of the verticle slats of the footboard.

In a few weeks, when I turn the Victorian clock on the nightstand back an hour, I will be finished with the saving of daylight for another year. But all the sunlight I have accumulated these past six months will not help illuminate one fall morning, nor can it allow one to postpone what is to come.

By October, when I return from my office in the late afternoon, it will be in the dark. Crickets still signal their cryptic messages from deep within the boxwood, but they will grow more faint until all that is left is the silence.

A short time later, birch trees will release yellowed leaves. The last of the rose petals will have fallen. They soon turn the color of ancient newspaper. A damp chill will replace the cool breeze that just weeks ago filtered through the open window leading to the garden.

Yet, about this time each year I begin to feel a profound restfulness in this place. The silence makes possible a special kind of gratitude for what has been. Having a sense of kindnesses bestowed, a sense for beautiful but transient gifts, is something given us by the fall.

Life in the garden is giving way to a thousand improbable accidents until the sum total of those events is a design, but it is a design for death. Still, the fall leaves the faintest hint of promise: there are those birds who remain. They are a remnant to remind us of the gift of summer. They are a remnant to remind us, as Rilke does, that only we comprehend flowering and fading simultaneously.

Baltimore Evening Sun, September, 1986.

Annual Lamps

Life in a modern city is full of chance sights and random associations, disappearing into infinity before their implications can fully be grasped. In our minds, these small incidents become stitched together with thread so fine that one's view of any great city becomes of a single piece. The seams between these events disappear or at least go undetected, making them more like music which can never be halted or fully examined at any paticular moment than a series of discreet happenings with clearly delineated beginnings and conclusions.

Even the shortest journey in the London underground offers a clacking and jerking collection of instantaneous onomatopoeia and momentary encounters: a glance at scuffed shoes, a baby cries, the sight of hands grasping overhead knob and tight-coiled spring handles. I watch a lady's pulse on the wrist which squeezes the handle next to mine, eyes momentarily caught in an embarrassed meeting; across the car: hands, shoes, cigarette smoke, faces, advertisements, eyes, all forgotten, unless later summoned in a dream. Each car a kind of rolling convention of solipcists. We all labor under the illusion that the others are there simply for our bemused but furtive examination.

Above ground now. A van passes bearing the legend: Rolls and Co. Ltd., Guillotine Knife Griders, 4 Bleeding Heart Yard. I want to think this one over, but the truck is gone, replaced by a street on which I find two shops facing each other. On the northeast corner: the Annual Lamp Company, across the way, Glass Benders.

Wait. There seems to be a complexity here beyond which Western civilization cannot go. The threads in my small cranium begin to become unraveled.

Annual Lamps. The mind boggles, the stitches have become completely undone. There seems no possible connection between these disparate words. It is infinitely stranger than the man in the subway tunnel playing *Mack the Knife* on a harmonica. Here the paradox has displayed itself on the space of a single, small sign.

Annual Lamps: so complicated it takes four strong men 12 months to make just one.

Annual Lamps -- people clearly gain their livelihoods from it. They pay their taxes and fill in the box marked 'occupation' "Annual Lamp maker: foreman" or "Annual Lamp maker: apprentice."

Annual Lamps: perhaps they change the entire work force once a year, the work being far too difficult and tedious for any mortal to last beyond that limit.

Annual Lamps: all of these interpretations dissolve, as I spy the other sign "Glass Benders." A rotund man with ballooned cheeks holds his blue faced breath in a large pipette until a disgruntling but familiar cracking sound is heard, followed by the unmistakable tinkle of defeated glass. He catches his breath while dejectedly pushing the straight broom which gathers the broken fragments off the shop floor. He will deposit them in a large, stainless steel vat. In a certain Sisyphusean fashion he will start again.

But Wait. The threads miraculously begin to reconnect. The shops are related. There is more here than an odd juxtaposition. One December afternoon, as the needle on the gauge mounts higher and higher, past the blue zone, all the way to the red "danger zone," the heavy man in the Osh-Gosh overalls turns bluer and bluer until. . . the glass does not crack.

Significant glances are exchanged with the supervisor, like

those traded by masked neurosurgeons in a starkly lit, green clad operating room.

In early December, the glass benders proudly, but carefully, carry the glass across the street to the waiting proprietors of the Annual Lamp Co.

"Well, mate, thought yawrn't going to make it this year."

Unpublished, February, 1983.

Intermolecular Spaces and Boardwalk Cracks

There is an almost surely apocryphal story of an eminent but elderly physicist who, in his later years, took to wearing enormous Alaskan snowshoes, as well as a 50-foot tether line anchored to one of the bed posts in his room at the retirement home.

He had, in his declining years, become afraid that he might fall through the infinitesimally small, but nonetheless real and abundant cracks and interstices of that largely empty molecular space the rest of us had spuriously come to call the real or natural world. What to others seemed like a leisurely stroll down the corridor to this aged scientist became a flirting with nonbeing -- something akin to the activities of an octogenarian tight-rope walker.

For him, this was the real world, and he had helped to describe it to the rest of us with access to university classrooms and scholarly journals. All about him, throughout the home, the other residents busied themselves with knitting, cards and checkers, not realizing that the checkers, like the players, leaped precariously from particle to particle over a series of yawning and bottomless abysses. In the meantime, the world outside the retirement home went about the takeover of the Falklands, a war in Lebanon, and in search of a balanced budget.

This summer, I became aware of another world, perhaps equally real and certainly a good bit more natural than the one I normally inhabit. It is a world that most of us, unfortunately, have begun to forget.

It all began on the boardwalk in Ocean City. The boardwalk: two and a half miles of quivering, quaking cellulite, fast-food places, and omnipresent displays of bad taste, running parallel to the Atlantic Ocean. All day long, and particularly after 5 p.m., people pound the boards, rarely turning their heads east toward the expansive ocean. Instead, their attention is inevitably riveted west, not on the setting sun, always breath-taking on the eastern shore this time of year, but rather in the direction of light sticks, mysterious dog leashes without canines, and the near-infinite expanse of pink, red and brown exposed flesh working its aimless way north and south.

As I sat on the beach one translucent afternoon, too late in the day for sun worshippers, I saw several small, spindly-legged birds playing a relentless game of give and take with the encroaching and receding surf. They were unconcerned about me. They were playing this curious game of aquatic tag with the prospect of acquiring dinner.

I sat very still in the shaft of sunlight that filtered through the spaces between the large hotels on the farther side of the boardwalk. To my surprise the birds came almost to my feet, sometimes with first course already in mouth. They were very small, beady-eyed and laboring under a misconception there was still harmony between their species and mine.

Behind me, other scavengers were at work -- an elderly couple, outfitted with metal detectors. Dressed identically, their baseball caps pulled down to what seemed like the tops of their baggy trousers, they held tightly to their methodically sweeping machines. They sifted through the sand in search of coins, keys and lost wedding rings. "Do you ever wonder about the stories that go with those lost rings?" "Never! It's their fault for being so careless."

On this pleasant shore a war seemed to exist that would continue until nothing remained but cellulite and metal detectors. Yet these strange little birds wanted very little: a slip of shore to scurry to and fro, a few morsels washed up from the deep. They are edge-of-the-world dwellers, caught between the vast, relentless ocean and Thrashers' french fries.

The birds now eyed me. As the metal detectors made another pass, I waved my arms frantically in the direction of the sandpipers. "Get out of here: you are in danger. These are cunning creatures who may hurt you." Then a thought seemed to cross their minds. Perhaps it was that the now setting sun had provided them with an unblinded view of the boardwalk. All at once, in perfect coordination, they lifted off, like several parts of a loosely constructed Japanese kite, and were gone.

With them went a piece of the natural world, perhaps the real world far from metal detectors and the assortment of tattoos and wallets chained to jeans just a few paces away. As I walked back to the boardwalk, I thought of another world not normally inhabited by sandpipers -- the world of hypercritical and analytic professors.

As I did, I checked my snowshoes; staring at the cracks between the boards, I held steadfastly to my tether line, which now seemed precariously tight and ready to break.

Baltimore Evening Sun, September, 1982.

Observing Aurora

For the last six months I have lived very peacefully across the hall from John, an unobtrusive and terribly polite Ph.D. student in applied mathematics. Every morning about 8:15 we nod to each other and trade half-hearted but obligatory "hellos" on our way to breakfast. Every now and then I even venture to attach a "John" to the end of my one word greeting, just so he knows I have not forgotten his name. He, on the contrary, never sullies his crisp and parsimonious salutation with any unnecessary syllables. Consequently, I have never heard John utter my name. At first, I could rationalize the omission by believing that he did not know my name. I soon remedied that situation by placing my name on the door, in block letters, squarely in the middle of a five by seven index card.

The morning following the completion of that task, I arose early in hopeful anticipation. But when I gave my usual greeting, adding a peculiar emphasis to the benevolent "John" I dangled at the end of my salutation, all I received in return was a quizzical look accompanied by the usual unenthusiastic "hello."

I have since resigned myself to the fact that since it is the case that my name contains two syllables, while John is a very easy to pronounce one, I would really be requiring him to do twice as much work in this relationship, and that would be morally reprehensible on my part.

What I do find strange about our relationship, however, if indeed it could properly be called that, is that although over the past six months I have exchanged about 400 words with this man (180 of them his), I always know where he is.

I have not been blessed with the gift of clairvoyance. In the place of a simple index card, on his door he has placed a two inch piece of adhesive tape on which is printed the not particularly startling Cartesian conclusion "I AM." He has neglected to include the very important premise Descartes thought necessary to arrive at the conclusion. Underneath these two words is placed a board on which are neatly penned a catalogue of 38 possible places John could be.

In addition to the place names, the board is also equipped with a movable red arrow that indicates the present answer to the mystery of John's whereabouts.

Included in his list are the usual places, the bathroom, bed, telephone box, dining room, common room, laundry and library. He also has a second category apparently related to work: math department, physics department, etc.

A third group of places John might be include the renaissance group, which is alotted four possible locations, the go-club in the computing lab, and perhaps the most impressive of all, "observing Aurora."

Additionally, John might also be found at several local addresses that he has carefully penned in at the bottom of the list. One of these undoubtedly is Aurora's house, where there is a sign affixed to the front door indicating the 38 possible places Aurora might be found--one of them, of course, is "observing John."

🐭 Unpublished, March, 1983.

Taking Christmas Too Seriously

There are individuals in each of our lives who are so much an integral part of the making of the people we have become that the very thought of these persons calls up images mixed with facts, and myth, symbol and magic.

These people represent something -- they stand for nearly forgotten childhoods, for losses of innocence. They are often tenuous but human embodiments of some important and essential principles by which we run our lives.

For me, John Das is one of these people -- those special people who, sometimes quite unwittingly, represent something larger than their individual lives.

The first impression of John Das was always his nose. It was an immense thing which hung between his large, dark eyes like a huge fleshy isosceles triangle. That nose, as well as the rest of his face, unless we have unwittingly fallen in the midst of a Gogol short story, is now living somewhere in the middle of his native India. For a few years we were classmates in graduate school.

By the end of his stay at my *alma mater,* John Das had accomplished a number of feats that, at least by some measure, might be considered quite remarkable: He was married in his backyard, next to the barbeque pit, to a nurse from Anne Arbor, Michigan. He had met her while in line at the supermarket. John Das was the first and last person to preach about Vishnu and Shiva from the pulpit of the university chapel. He once bounded down the steps of his adopted home and with two dollars left in his pocket hailed a taxi and in his Indian accent instructed the bewildered driver to, "Let me have two dollars worth." Along the way, he also managed to establish a school record for the number of incomplete courses in a single academic career.

John Das was one of those rare students who fairly early on realized that academic questions are often interlopers in a world where too few of the real ones ever get asked. In the sphere of graduate education John Das was an unmitigated flop. Yet he was one of those rare men who remained unspoiled by his failure. The reason I write about him is that I can no longer think about the Christmas season without first calling to mind his eccentric, peripatetic fellow with the big nose.

One morning, nearly a decade ago, just before our Christmas vacation, we began a rather animated conversation about why Americans become so excited about the holiday season. I remember indignantly quoting to him a line from John Andrew Holmes's *Wisdom in Small Doses:* "The Christmas season has come to mean the time when the public plays Santa Claus to the merchants." John Das, the devout Hindu, would have none of this.

The afternoon before, he had purchased from the local army/navy store a new olive green overcoat. As our discussion about the value of Christmas continued, we entered the queue for breakfast. As the line inched toward the hot food counter, we came in range of the stubble faced, alcoholic old man who often did odd jobs around the refectory in exchange for a hot cup of coffee and a warm spot to shake off the cold and loneliness of the streets for a few hours. The man had managed to survive six decades of this planet; his deeply lined face looked more like the countenance of a man of 80. John Das, in characteristic fashion, gave him a warm greeting and the man, looking as ashen and unredeemed as Marley's ghost, complimented the Indian on his new coat.

After breakfast, John Das disappeared for a few moments. When he returned, he was without the overcoat. He had given it to the old man. As we began to walk home, I berated him for giving away the coat. I phrased it the way philosophy graduate students sometimes do: That taking too much upon oneself is not a moral requirement. John Das mostly smiled as a response, his white teeth matching the buttons on his red cotton shirt and the frozen snow piled high on either side of the sidewalk. Moments later, we were stopped by a mutual friend who inquired if John Das was not cold without a jacket in the 20 degree weather. "Only on the outside," was his reply. The friend moved on, realizing, I suspect, he had just been used in illustrating a point.

I nevertheless continued my questioning as we resumed our walk. I successfully pointed out all the possible psychological causes for his act of benevolence. After several more moments of his smiling silence, we arrived at the corner where we were to part company. After toeing the crusted snow with one alligator shoe, he finally looked at me with those clear, dark eyes, like two pieces of coal ready to be put in my stocking. In a calm but clear voice he said, "You know, you are probably right. I think my problem is I take your Christmas too seriously."

Baltimore Evening Sun, December, 1984.

Margaret Mead: Who Fells This Redwood?

I have just finished reading a book that is, at least indirectly, about Margaret Mead. It was published after her recent death, but in some ways, it attempts to dig her up, so that a curious kind of matricide might be performed.

The essential thesis of this new work is that Mead was incorrect in many of her observations about Samoans in the late 1920's. This new publication does not argue she was inaccurate about a few minor details. The thesis is that she was dead wrong about many of the most important elements of Samoan life.

This brings me to the crux of these comments. All too often in the academic life these days we seem to lose a sense of humility and respect for those intellectuals who have come before us. I have no stake in defending Mead. I might have wished for the body to have been a little colder before it was exhumed, but I am more concerned with the way in which we point out the errors of those who have preceded us, particularly if those individuals criticized are seen as important figures in their respective fields.

Sir Isaac Newton once remarked that if he saw farther than others it was because he stood on the shoulders of giants. Presumably, he was speaking of Copernicus, Galileo, Tycho, Kepler, Francis Bacon, and other brilliant thinkers who, because of the passing of time and the workings of other adept minds, proved to be wrong about a great number of important things.

What Newton clearly appreciated, however, is something that seems to be lost these days in the world of scholarship: these people were wrong, but they were brilliantly wrong. Even Newton, after his early discoveries in optics, cosmology and physics, went on to write some 600,000 words on alchemy and related topics. These manuscripts seem a little silly and incongruous when placed alongside his earlier works, but they still on occasion contain genuine insights about chemical theory and the nature of elements, not to mention the human condition.

These days, reputations in the academic life seem too often to be made by the felling of intellectual redwoods. If one is to make a name in the academic world, it is often at the expense of another. Unfortunately, in the process of felling these intellectual giants, we often show ourselves as termites. Recently, during one of my classes I made what I believed was a fairly innocuous comment about Freud and psychoanalysis. This remark brought an unexpected series of gutteral sounds from a young woman seated in the first row.

"Freud was a jerk," she sputtered, "he hated women." Scholars these days are, of course, busily at work on Freud's alleged mysogny, but what is disturbing about this exchange is that this young person of 19 or 20 had blithely attempted to sum up the life of one of the greatest thinkers in Western intellectual history in two short sentences. When I inquired as to which of Freud's works she found most offensive, the young woman responded by saying that people like that are not worth reading.

It is Soren Kierkegaard who reminds us that lives can always be understood backwards, the trouble is they have to be lived forwards. There is no doubt Freud's attitude about women could have been considerably better, but he lived in a Victorian age -- an era when his attitude differed little from those of other Western European men of his time. We have the luxury of looking back on Freud's life, he was too busy living it.

We could, of course, tell a similar tale about Charles Darwin, Karl Marx, Max Weber, Paul Tillich, Bertrand Russel, I.F.

Stone's latest *ad hominem* arguments against the character of Socrates, or any number of other intellectual giants whom smaller men and women seem to be so busy killing these days.

All of these comments bring me back to Newton. Edward Gibbon, no intellectual pygmy by anyone's measure, once remarked that he was proud to belong to the same species as Sir Isaac Newton.

And it was Newton, this intellectual titan who described himself as standing on the shoulders of giants - men he was fully aware were sometimes thoroughly wrong. No wonder he saw so far. Perhaps the reason our vision is often not nearly so good is that it is so difficult to see a great distance when standing on a redwood stump.

🍎 *Baltimore Evening Sun,* April, 1983.

Loneliness

I have just been for a walk by myself to a secret spot. It lies up the coast from St. Andrews in a part of the Scottish shore where a single, stubborn nub of land juts out defiantly into a giant, dark and cold North Sea. I have only traveled to this spot at night, usually on pleasant, cloud-strewn evenings where stars make few dim and fleeting appearances. Although I have been there many times before I had never really noticed before this evening just how lonely a place it is. Tonight all the proper ingredients were present: a fluorescent and unusually tranquil sea, the benign crescent of a moon, a barely detectable inland breeze which brought the sounds of a far removed city.

I was feeling lonely, so I took the walk. The beauty of it all made me lonelier. There is something about beautiful places seen at night that seems to affect my sad feelings in much the same way a hollow dome transforms music, making it enormously resonant, enabling it to possess me completely.

It is the great silence that makes the secret spot so overwhelmingly lonely. Seagulls bed down for the night in tiny crags and clumps of straw colored grass that hang by sturdy little roots, like the grasping fingers of frightened children, to the sheer face of a starkly vertical cliff which takes an abrupt plunge to the sea. The birds have ended their gliding search for food until first light. The sleeping gulls are my only companions. On this night, at that place, I share the secret beauty with no other, I have been made a solitary creature.

Only lately have I come to realize there are two varieties of loneliness. This evening, for the first time I have understood they are wedded to two kinds of silence. The first kind of loneliness happens only when people are around. It is a loneliness that requires humans to be as sociable as pigeons. It often occurs when I am feeling lonely and desperately try to overcome it by searching out another kindred soul. The usual result is that we make each other even lonelier. Often this is not an admission easily made, thus we sleep together in our collective loneliness.

The other variety of loneliness can only be experienced by the secret self. It is the kind of solitary state where the nearly forgotten dead come forth from their graves. They are real enough to be remembered, they are phantom enough that they cannot or will not dispel the loneliness. It is a state of mind that forces one to take notice of the past and the future. It is the kind of loneliness that allows one, uninterrupted, to add and subtract the years, to focus on long forgotten moments, to make promises to the self, never made with the tongue, but always kept with the heart. What one experiences in this brand of loneliness is not solitude, but it is, I think, a step along the way.

Each kind of loneliness is accompanied by its own brand of silence. In the one kind, the silence found at the secret place, no words are ever spoken. The sense of sound becomes extraneous. In the other loneliness, the one with others, a torrent of language is unleashed in a vain attempt at overcoming separation. At the secret spot, I am left with the overwhelming feeling of nakedness. In the loneliness with others, I begin to feel like a bag person, several pieces of bulky, ill-fitting clothing isolating me from the rest of the world. In this kind of loneliness speech becomes so many layers of smelly woolen garments worn to hide my nakedness.

It is only the kind of silence experienced at the secret spot that is worth possessing, for it has the possibility of moving one through loneliness to solitude. It is this kind of silence where, if the world becomes just still enough, an inner voice may be heard. It tells me important things. It tells me that loneliness is sometimes desireable. It whispers that solitude is possible.

🐭 Unpublished, October, 1985.

Caught Underwears

Someone threw a boulder through the left-rear window of my car the other evening. I had been giving a series of lectures at a local church on the problem of evil. Just about the time Job was being given a new collection of sheep and a better set of children, outside on the parking lot, I was losing some old pairs of underwear.

The rector of the church found the large flat rock sitting on the back seat of my car after one of the parishers had noticed the broken glass spread over the parking lot.

When we arrived at the car, my book bag full of philosophical tracts and student papers was still on the front seat. It had been searched through but nothing was missing. A large bag of apples, navel oranges, and seedless grapes had also been left untouched. What had disappeared was a big blue canvas bag full of freshly laundered shorts and socks.

In all there must have been ten pairs of underwear and perhaps a dozen pairs of socks. The following morning I felt quite like the proverbial child who was warned by his mother to always wear clean underpants because you never know when you might be hit by a bus and taken to the hospital.

If the truth be known I was more than a bit embarrassed by my underwear. It was unfashionably white and, after extensive wear, had begun to suffer from effects of gravity. Consequently, every pair that went into the making of the larceny tended to be rather droopy in the front and baggy in the behind.

My socks were really no better. Most of the pairs nearly matched, not only in color, but also in terms of the holes.

When the policeman arrived at the scene of the crime he gave me a complaint number and in an attempt to bolster my spirits he said, "You never know when you might have something more to report about the crime." After telling me to "keep your eye peeled for the stolen goods" he asked me to describe the contents of the bag. I had an urge to make my underwear sound a little more interesting than it was, but I resisted. It is something akin, I should think, to the guilt and embarrassment felt by children wearing dirty underwear and holey socks who are hit by buses and taken to the hospital.

For the better part of the following day my conscience continued to bother me. I decided to visit various health clubs and shoe stores in the hopes of identifying my underpants and/or socks and making a proper apology to the thief for the shoddy condition of the stolen goods. It is only in such places where one can stare at underwear and socks without people getting the wrong idea.

But after hanging around a downtown health club for the better part of the morning I came to the painful realization of just how dilapidated my jockey shorts were. Everyone at the club was walking around the locker room in very spiffy and not in the least bit baggy or droopy multicolored underwear. This made me so embarrassed and guilt stricken I decided I could not face the thief even if he were to show up.

So, I've decided to rectify the situation by taking out a personal ad and inviting the thief to steal my other blue canvas bag which I will fill with brand new socks and spiffy, bright colored, interesting looking jockey shorts. I have kept the boulder, (it's still sitting on the backseat), and by then the left rear window should be fixed. The ad will read something like this:

SWM (that's me) desires UT (that's him) for the purpose of substituting more presentable undergarments. Experience necessary. No new equipment needed. Reply immediately.

I know now disappointed the thief must be. I hope he allows me to make it up to him.

🍎 *Baltimore Evening Sun,* April, 1985.

*R*eaders *of Messages*

Homo Sapiens. We are the great readers of messages. This penchant for divination probably began the day the first perplexed human gazed into a still pond and saw a bewildered visage staring back. We seem always to be discerning meanings in a world in which our cats and dogs quite easily participate without even the slightest desire for the contemplation of what it all means. Perhaps that is why the dogs at my house don't read the entrails of the birds they kill. They also never look skyward on a star-filled evening only to find the outlines of themselves, as well as a variety of outsized kitchen utensils, blazing in the infinite night.

We humans regularly compress reality down to a manageable size, successful in neatly placing it within the confines of a crystal ball, the flat surface of a ouija board, or the parameters of a periodic table of the elements, all curious but understandable attempts at domesticating the mysterious, and perhaps the terrible.

I have come to believe this searching for messages goes a long way in explaining why human beings are the only animals who suffer from insomnia. The night is the best time for the search. The darkness provides a silent background for reading the messages found. The dogs lose no sleep over these matters. They seem always to rest comfortably for they are unaware of their tremendous smallness. We humans are also tiny specks of protoplasm when measured against the whole of it, but we are self-conscious specks, a blessing, and sometimes a curse, brought to us by four billion years of evolution and the hand of the Divine.

We human beings are like mice scurrying to and fro in the pyramid tombs of Cheops and Chepren. But the difference between ourselves and the rest of the animals lies in our realization we are mice. The raccoons who regularly raid my trash cans have dark deepset eyes in their masked faces. They live, as we do, in a world poised precariously between two near-infinite universes, one microscopic, one telescopic, and, thanks to Galileo, both crying out to be viewed. But the neurons and synapses do a much less inquisitive dance in their tiny fur-lined brains. They seem to fret very little about the cosmos out there, or the one within.

The squirrels on my property are marvelously and efficiently wired for life. The existential questions seem never to enter their 16 ounces worth of grey matter. This may have something to do with the fact that none of these creatures seems to share our fascination and fear of the dark. The animals sleep. The night is for humans to ask the unanswerable questions.

Darkness. It is such a mysterious thing. It is not something with which most of us are terribly comfortable. Our cro-magnon cousins, judging by their fire-lit caves, seem to have shared our conviction about its mystery. Indeed, it may well be the case that one way to tell the story of the history of civilization is by carefully cataloguing the advances in man's attempts at illuminating the night.

The inscription inside Samuel Johnson's watch is reported to have read: THE NIGHT COMETH. Friedrick Froebel, a 19th century German literary critic once wrote, "It is only the conviction that it is the darkness within us that makes the darkness without that can restore the lost peace in our souls." As children, most of us, I should think, begin dimly to understand the convictions expressed by Johnson and Froebel. Until the age of seven, I refused to venture into the basement after dark without first switching on the light. When I arrived with some trepidation at the bottom of the steps, the few seconds of new illumination had always managed to dispel whatever it was that lived down there in the dark.

It is only in retrospect I understand why I was not to find them, even if I raced to the bottom of the stairs. It was not that they did not exist. It was because I carried them around with me. It was only in the dark I remembered they were there.

These days, my demons are a little more obvious, perhaps the result of the accumulated effort in my adult years to make conscious what was formerly deeply embedded in my soul. But the ability to possess one's own demons is something that only we, *homo sapiens,* seem to have. It is a blessing. It is a curse. It comes with being a reader of messages.

Unpublished, January, 1978.

The Self-Advertisement Hall of Fame

Summer has softened me, and I have been able to flop down on my couch for the last couple of weeks to watch some television. What I found didn't come as much of a surprise. The networks are serving up the same stuff they were this time last year: a bunch of cops with lots of hair on their chests chasing around bad guys who are always terrible drivers; game shows in which outsized letters are turned by slinky blonds, while contestants jump up and down with advanced cases of greed written on their faces; nightime soap operas featuring nasty, jewel-laden women suffering from a strange and incurable combination of mean-spiritedness and overactive hormones.

What my viewing has taught me in the last few weeks is that some of the best acting on television is to be found in commercials. Some of the more distinguished of these performances are by business and professional people who appear on the tube to sell their own goods and services. Ambulance chasers, automobile executives, hair weave shop keepers, presidents of electric razor companies, mayors wanting to be governor, people hawking tires, chicken moguls, owners of ice cream factories, trendy cosmetic sellers and newspaper publishers, all are getting in the act.

Of course, some of these performances are better than others. There are enough self-advertisers around these days that it is clear we will soon need some way of recognizing the most accomplished of these actors, some process of winnowing out the good from the not-so-good.

So I'd like to suggest we raise some funds for a "Self-Advertisement Hall of Fame" to recognize the very best of these performances. We could begin with a modest building, eventually perhaps expanding the hall to become one of the larger city attractions.

It goes without saying that Manny, Moe and Jack, the Pep Boys, should be the first inductees. Although they have rarely appeared on television, they should still be recognized for their achievements in other media, particularly billboards and radio. And they accomplished this self-advertisement, I might add, while laboring under the handicap of vast numbers of people believing they are the Three Stooges. We know now, of course, the Pep Boys are not the Three Stooges: they are your car's three best friends. I like the fact they are not even remotely interested in getting to know me. It is with my car they wish to have a meaningful relationship, a sort of motorized *menage a quatre.* This is reason enough to make them our first inductees.

Along with the Pep Boys, we should also think about giving Mr. Ray a life achievement award in self-advertisement. His hair weave commercials, with the now familiar "Hi, I'm Mr. Ray," remain classics in the field. The "before pictures" -- aerial views of barren, lonely heads looking like miniature helicopter landing pads, and the "after" shots of thick-haired couples dancing cheek to cheek while Mr. Ray, discreetly in the background, watches approvingly, probably will never be surpassed. I have always been fond of Mr. Ray's advertisements because he usually stands off to the side, never the center of attention. He acts as a kind of omniscient narrator in his commercials, while avoiding the temptation to become a *deus ex machina.* His approach to self-advertisement is clearly the stuff of which the hall of fame should be made.

The other possible charter member is Mr. Carvel of Carvel ice cream fame. Despite decades of commercials, he has remained a disembodied voice from somewhere in southern New Jersey. He obviously understood long ago that having to look at the body that goes with that voice might permanently turn people off to ice cream. He lets his voice do all the work, wisely choosing to show his ice cream, rather than himself, to the viewers.

This illustrious group, the Pep Boys, Mr. Ray, and the Carvel ice cream man, needs to be recognized and thus distinguished from the inferior performances of ambulance chasers playing trivial pursuit, ambulance chasers demonstrating whiplash, and ambulance chasers standing alongside smoking hulks of steel that used to be somebody's family sedan. The hall of famers need to be set apart from men who suffer from strange, existential dilemmas by calling themselves Mr. Nobody. We must distinguish Manny, Moe and Jack from chicken salesmen who mistakenly believe we like them as much as their hens do.

The distinction must clearly be shown between Mr. Ray and elected city officials who sit in their city hall offices in the dead of night making television commercials about how they sit in their city hall offices in the dead of night. Presumably, during the day they are too busy thinking about what it would be like to place signs all over the state proclaiming that this particular park bench or that particular trash can or rest stop urinal has been brought to you by the governor and the citizens of the state of Maryland.

Above all, we want to honor the hall of famers for their honesty. They should be formally recognized so as never to be confused with self-advertisers like the guy in the bathrobe who swears he bought the electric razor company because he liked the shave he got. Everybody knows he bought the company so he could be in his own television commercials.

Baltimore Evening Sun, July, 1986.

*M*undane Mysteries

There is a large manilla folder in the file cabinet of my office. It is marked "Mysteries, mundane." The contents of the file are not related to the more profound unresolved questions of life: Does God exist? Is there an answer to the problem of evil? How much did the president know and when? The mysteries contained in that folder are of the everyday variety. For the past several years, I have jotted down small notes to myself in an attempt to keep track of them.

As a child, I also struggled to keep tabs on various conundrums, large and small. Few of those have accompanied me into adulthood. By the age of seven or eight, I understood only too well the regrettable answer to how Santa Claus could be in so many places at the same time. By 10 or 11, it was clear why I was caught whenever engaged in some wrongful activity. My mother possessed a somewhat specialized but highly serviceable kind of omniscience with respect to my whereabouts. There were other mysteries left unresolved: Why church-going girls in my grade school class bobby-pinned Kleenex to the tops of their heads when they had forgotten or misplaced the beanies they were required to wear; why intelligent, god-fearing nuns in my grade school thought bobby-pinning Kleenex to the top of the heads of eight and nine year old girls was a good idea; what God must have thought looking down from those infinite heights at the tops of the heads of eight and nine year old girls covered in Kleenex, so as not to offend Him.

In adulthood, the questions became more complex, the answers as elusive and inaccessible as a fly's home. For some years now, I have made my living teaching philosophy. As a function of my employment, I have engaged in asking and attempting to answer many of the more vexing questions life poses. I use the word "attempt" in the previous sentence not out of a feeling of false modesty, but rather from a sense of reverence for the mystery and profundity of the questions I am allowed to ponder in the everyday course of my job. I receive a paycheck every two weeks for thinking in the day time about important questions that keep many thoughtful people wide awake in the middle of the night.

Still, there is the manilla folder marked "Mysteries, mundane" in my file cabinet. As I said earlier, the items in the folder are not of the cosmic variety. I bring up these everyday mysteries now, for I have a vague but fervent hope someone may know the answers. This might reduce the size of the file marked "Mysteries, mundane," so that the folder might have a little more breathing room between "Mysore" and "Mysticism." I offer these ten conundrums in no particular order. They appear here as they were randomly retrieved from the file.

When attending a concert or movie, what are the rules for who gets the arm rests? Is it first come, first served? Are people suppose to share? Does each patron get the one to the left? Clearly this last suggestion is not workable, for the person seated on the right aisle would have the undeserved benefit of two arm rests. Perhaps theatres could include an announcement about who has legitimate claim to the arm rests along with the reminder that in case of fire we should walk, not run, to the nearest exit.

What is the opposite of having a "personal opinion?" Is it having an "impersonal opinion?" Is it possessing someone else's opinion? When people say, "It's my personal opinion," why do they put the world "only" between "it's" and "my?" It smacks of a kind of insecurity people who go around talking about "personal opinions" don't generally have.

Why do people use the expression, "Still waters run deep?" By their very nature still waters don't run, they don't walk, they don't even crawl. It should be obvious, if they are genuinely still waters, all they do is sit there.

Why do swanky restaurants I have seen in Florida post signs outside which read: NO GUIDE DOGS ALLOWED? For whom are those signs intended? Blind people can't see, and dogs can't read. I've often wondered if these restaurants in the past might have had a problem with vacationing or retired sherpas trying to bring their pack dogs to lunch.

Why do men's dress shirts always come with 24 pins sticking them to pieces of white cardboard? Why are there never a couple of dozen pins sticking women's blouses to pieces of cardboard? Is there some danger men's shirts may wander off? Are they naturally more active than women's blouses? Or do women's blouses practice more self-control?

Why do waiters and waitresses always tell me their first names? They do the same thing every time. They rush up to the table, napkins draped over their arms, crooked bow ties and black aprons in place, and exclaim, "Hi, I'm Tina, and I'm going to be your waitress this evening." What are the other possibilities for why Tina could be dressed that way and hanging around in a restaurant? Why do I always feel so guilty and unsociable when I don't introduce myself after Tina has broken the ice? "Hi, I'm Stephen, and I'm going to be your customer this evening."

Why do people always stare at the floor or gaze at the numbers blinking overhead whenever they occupy an elevator? Why do they never look at the three other walls or the other people in the elevator? Why do people in crowded elevators always hold their breath? Is there something about the air in crowded elevators the rest of us should know?

Why do people take candy wrapped in cellophane to the symphony? Why does it take these people a full five minutes to unwrap each piece? Is there a certain kind of palsy that comes with the long term ingestion of candy wrapped in cellophane? Why do these candies always come individually wrapped? Why don't these people with candy palsy unwrap their treats before the concert, between movements, or at the intermissions?

Why do hot dogs come ten to a pack, while hot dog rolls can only be purchased with eight in a package? One has to buy four packs of hot dogs and five bags of rolls just to make it all work out. When you live alone, this creates a tremendous problem of leftovers. Why has it become increasingly difficult to find 39 friends willing to come over for leftover hot dogs?

What are the buttons for that can be found on electrical poles at crosswalks? I have never seen one when pushed that had any discernible effect on the changing of the traffic lights. Why do people stand there and frantically push them anyway? Is there some sort of strange placebo affect at work here? It deserves some mention that rats who have had 95 percent of their brains surgically removed will soon stop pushing the lever after they discover it no longer leads to the acquisition of food pellets.

This last mundane mystery leads me to ask an 11th and final questions: Why do rates who have had 95 percent of their brains surgically removed frequently appear to be more intelligent than human beings? This is clearly not one of the mundane mysteries. It belongs in a file marked "Mysteries, Profound."

🐛 Unpublished, December, 1986.

At Last, Renewal

Late last evening, a wedge of barking geese brought me out of a deep sleep. At first, while still submerged below the deep ripples of unconsciousness, I feared the sounds were made by menacing, deep-throated dogs voicing their displeasure at me. But when the room finally came into focus, I realized the distant barking was the sound of geese returning home.

It was the first real sign of spring. I don't think I have yet seen a crocus -- those flowers Emily Dickinson called spring's first conviction. I have had no real time to check for buds opening on the beech trees just inside the gate. But spring is sooner recognized by plants than by humans.

After awakening, I stood among the boxwood and watched the score of perfectly choreographed birds pass a clear and silent moon. The sky was full of golden sequins, resting on a background of deep purple, nearly black.

For the past several weeks, I had given a series of Lenten talks on the concept of "miracles." The lectures were quite scholarly -- exploring ideas of some of the best philosophical minds the Western tradition has to offer. The talks were supposed to help the listeners to understand the miracle of Easter. But in those weeks, the seeds of Easter, the stuff of which resurrection is made, had not yet germinated in my soul.

Last evening, I continued to gaze at the stars after the geese had disappeared into the otherwise silent night. In the winter months, the stars look cold. In December and January, the stars are almost always silent, mute, unfeeling. Last evening, they were like the first guests arriving at a splendid party. They had decided, while at home dressing, that they would spend the entire night dancing. In winter, gazing at the heavens reminds me I am made of the dust of the earth. Last evening, on the cusp of spring, a few days before Easter, I was convinced my stuff is the dust of the stars.

One cannot and should not speak of these things in lectures about miracles. Yet, every year at this time, this same miracle of transformation blossoms somewhere deep in my chest. Winter may have brought serious doubts about God, the self and its possibility for resurrection. But in the spring, doubt gives way to confirmation. I am given, in the Easter season, the capacity to perceive the abiding in the transitory, the invisible in the visible. In January, I am more than anything else, an unutterable sigh. But in the spring, just as Lent is coming to a close, there is a final triumph of faith over incongruity.

Last evening, the stars reminded me of the physicist's observation that the universe is more like a thought than anything else. Easter is the time, more than any other, which requires of me the belief that there exists the mind of an Eternal Thinker.

Baltimore Evening Sun, March, 1986.